EXETER GIRLS

LETTERS FROM
A FEEBLE-MINDED SCHOOL

VOLUME I

ISBN 978-0-9825049-3-2

theladdschool.com

Exeter Girls

BY JASON R. CARPENTER

CANNO

.I.

CONTENTS.

Some names have been changed to obfuscate the identities
of individuals acknowledged in this book.

		Upper
Lower Plate		
Cleaning		
Teeth Ext.	X	

Exeter Girls

Less than a century ago, it was widely accepted by conventional science that feeble-mindedness was one of the greatest threats to society in the modern era. But while hereditary diseases or defects of the mind and body were most commonly associated with feeble-mindedness, it was not defined by cognitive, intellectual or physical ability alone - morality and sexuality were traits equally as culprit in its diagnosis, and believed to be just as inheritable by birth.

The procreation of the feeble-minded was therefore considered not only the principal causative factor in the proliferation of disease, but vice, crime, and poverty, as well. And so the notion that there existed a link between immorality and genetic inferiority was brought to bear upon the reproductive rights of disadvantaged women everywhere.

For this reason, from 1911 through the Great Depression, hundreds of impoverished and uneducated young girls and women from broken homes, orphanages, jail cells, psychiatric hospitals, convents, and maternity wards across Rhode Island were legally declared feeble-minded and committed indefinitely to an institution for the mentally retarded.

The Wide and The Narrow Way

Once committed to the feeble-minded school there were few ways, and still fewer chances, for a girl or young woman to reclaim her liberty, let alone her good name. Above all else, trust had to be earned - of the institution's doctor, the head matron, and the social worker - through chastity, labor and obedience. Typically, this would entail many years of training and confinement before the notion would be so much as entertained that a woman, institutionalized for her sexual delinquency, could be permitted to return to the community on even a trial basis.

Every effort was therefore made in the superintendent's strict judgment to ensure that such women prove, while confined at the school, they could lead free lives as celibate, productive members of society. Any deviance from the same would otherwise necessitate they remain legally confined at the institution against their will at least until after menopause, and sometimes for the rest of their lives.

For some girls, the despair of knowing this was their fate inspired them to take drastic measures; but for many others, there was no other way out.

EVELYN

Fifteen years old. Mental age nine. Walks, talks, tidy. American. Episcopalian. Moron. Reads and writes. Immoral behavior. Sex promiscuity. Has had one illegitimate child. Stubborn, indifferent, inattentive. Indolent at times. Talks like an ordinary child. Settlement obtained in Newport, Rhode Island. Committed by the First District Court. Five brothers. Two sisters. Paternal cousin had to be married to a Portuguese. Paternal uncle a heavy drinker. Father a heavy drinker; supposed to have committed suicide by drowning. Mother inclined to beg from many sources.

January 1, 1915

My dear Dr. Ladd:

I am about to leave Newport and Miss Thomas is taking charge of the case of Evelyn Cook, and hoping to have her soon go to you. This work at the hospital will be carried on by Miss Jean King of Washington, who I hope will have the pleasure soon of visiting your school. We have the blanks also for the boy of whom I wrote you, who is still a patient here and with whom the doctors have not yet decided what is the best thing to do.

   Wishing you and Mrs. Ladd a very happy year in 1915, I remain,

Very truly yours,
Ellen Taylor
Social Service Department, Newport Hospital

January 5, 1915

My Dear Miss Taylor,

Your note received in regard to Evelyn Cook, and will say in reply that this girl may be brought to the school as soon as you have obtained the statement of her settlement in Rhode Island from Honorable Walter S. Blackmar, State House, Providence, RI.

Very truly yours,
Dr. Joseph H. Ladd, Supt.

January 8, 1915

Dear Sir: -

Evelyn Cook, an applicant to the School for Feeble-Minded at Exeter
and now a resident of Newport is justly chargeable to the State of Rhode
Island. This is the case that Miss Thomas is interested in.

Very truly yours,
Walter R. Blackmar
Agent of State Charities and Corrections

April 12, 1915

My dear Mrs. Cook:

Enclosed you will find the letter which you sent to Evelyn on April 7th. I did not give this letter to Evelyn, because I feel that it would only serve to make her discontented an unhappy. It is very much better, in your letters to Evelyn, to make no reference whatever to her coming home; or to her getting work outside of the institution. If you have anything of this sort that you wish to say, please write to me, instead of to Evelyn.

Also, it does not add to her happiness to emphasize too strongly your misfortunes, or those of her friends and relatives. It is much better for you to write her a cheerful letter, even though you do not feel that you have much grounds for doing so.

I am glad to tell you that Evelyn is in excellent physical condition.

Very truly yours,
Dr. Joseph H. Ladd, Supt.

May 25, 1915

Mrs. Cook,

2 pr. shoes, size 7
3 nightgowns, size 34 in. bus meas.
6 pr. stockings, size 10
4 pr. drawers, size 30 in.

You are requested to send the above things to Evelyn.

Very truly yours,
Dr. Joseph H. Ladd, Supt.

June 30, 1915

To Dr. Ladd,

Dear sir,

I telephoned the other day to ask you if you would be willing to please let Evelyn come home for a week's vacation as I would like to have her very much. Hoping to hear from you soon. If you wish to telephone me my number is 2252, Mrs. Owens, the lady I work for.

Yours sincerely,
Mrs. Loretta Cook

July 1, 1915

My dear Mrs. Cook,

In reply to you letter of June 30, I would say that you may take your daughter home for a week if you so desire.

Very truly yours,
Dr. Joseph H. Ladd, Supt.

July 2, 1915

To Dr. Ladd

Dear sir,

I thank you very much for letting Evelyn home as I would be very glad to see her after so long. Are you willing to let her stay a week? I am sending two dollars and you can tell Evelyn to order what you wish.

Yours sincerely,
Mrs. Loretta Cook

July 3, 1915

Dear Mrs. Cook:

Permit me to say that Evelyn may remain with you till July 10th, if you wish.

Very truly yours,
Dr. Joseph H. Ladd, Supt.

July 5, 1915

To Dr Ladd

Dear sir,

I hold myself responsible if anything happens to Evelyn either on the train or boat, as I cannot get off. But the lady says Evelyn can stay with me while she is here.

Yours sincerely,
Mrs. L Cook

November 12, 1915

To Dr. Ladd

Dear sir,

I now write these few lines to you about the boys. Of course every time I
write to Evelyn I ask her how the boys are. I received a letter from her and
she said she had not seen them for four weeks. I wish you would please be
kind to do me a great kindness to let the two little boys see Evelyn either
once a week or every two weeks as I feel very anxious about them, as they
are so young to be so far away from me. I hope they are well and getting
along nicely. I have sent Evelyn some clothes and hope you will find them
suitable for her to wear. I will try to get up and see them soon. I am glad
Evelyn is getting along nicely as she seems to be fond of the laundry.

Sincerely yours,
Mrs. Loretta Cook

November 16, 1915

My dear Mrs. Cook:-

I beg to acknowledge receipt of your note of November 12th concerning
Evelyn and the little boys. In reply permit me to say that they are all in
good health, and that the boys continue to enjoy their life here very greatly.
It is evident that they have not had opportunity previously to get out of
doors and work and play in the dirt, as both of the boys are very fond of
this, and get a great deal of satisfaction and pleasure out of it.

In regard to the visiting between and Evelyn and the boys, permit me
to say that we have a great many children under our care and many thing
to think about. For this reason we do not hold ourselves responsible to
see that the children visit. Evelyn has been told that she can see the boys
occasionally if she asks to do so, but if she does not I am afraid we cannot
see that she does it.

The little boys are not in school or class work at present, as our classes are
not started yet. There has been no special emphasis on the class work with
both boys as previous experience has proven that it is by far more desirable
to teach our children to do some kind of work than it is to spend too
much time on their reading and writing as they are not able to progress far
enough with their academic vocation to be of any particular value to them
in later life, while the ability to do some kind of work is of great value to
them. I do not mean by this that we shall not try to teach them to read and
write and to do number work, but that we shall consider the other work of
very much greater importance.

Very truly yours,
Dr. Joseph H. Ladd, Supt.

December 9, 1915

To Dr Ladd

Dear sir,

I now write these few lines to you asking you if you will please be kind
enough to let Evelyn home for the Christmas holidays about a week or ten
days as I would very much like to have her. I will be responsible for her
safety there and back. Ethel, Timothy and William are well and getting
along nicely. Do you think they are contented?

Sincerely yours,
Mrs. L. Cook

December 11, 1915

My dear Mrs. Cook:-

I beg to acknowledge your note of December 9th. In reply permit me to say
that we do not allow our children to go home for visits during the winter,
as we have found from experience it is not best to do so. On this account I
am returning the letter you wrote to Evelyn. I thought it best, as long as she
could not go home, that she knew nothing about it for it would only make
her discontented and unhappy.

Very truly yours,
Dr. Joseph H. Ladd, Supt.

December 13, 1915

To Dr. Ladd

Dear sir,

I have secured a splendid position for my daughter Evelyn. I have therefore decided to take her home.

I have seen Dr. Potter concerning this matter and he agreed with my plans.

I hope to hear from you concerning this matter in the near future. I think that Evelyn is just as capable of fulfilling the requirements of this position as she now is working free of charge for the State. This would be of great help to me. I beg to remain,

Yours truly,
Mrs. L Cook

December 18, 1915

My dear Mrs. Cook:-

I beg to acknowledge your note of December 13th concerning Evelyn.
In reply I beg to urge you to consider very seriously before taking Evelyn
home and putting her out anywhere to work.

  Of course you cannot fail to realize that Evelyn is not like the ordinary
girl, and has not the ability and judgment to govern herself and take care
of herself that the ordinary girls has. For this reason she should not be
subjected to the trials and temptations of life that is perfectly right for
other girls to be. Evelyn has not the judgment to decide what she should
do in case anyone asks her to do any particular thing. The great danger
in Evelyn's case, as in the case with other girls like her, is that she will get
into sexual difficulties, if she is out in the world. I have had many years'
experience with these girls and have known hundreds of them, and I very
strongly advise you to allow Evelyn to stay where she is. As you say Evelyn is
probably quite as capable to do the work you have selected for her to do as
she is to work here for the State of Rhode Island.

  I cannot blame you for feeling that the benefit of Evelyn's labor belongs
to you rather than to the State, but there is another side to the question.
In case Evelyn goes home and gets into trouble and had a child, who is
to support the child? Evelyn certainly is not capable of doing it, and in
that case it would fall upon you and you would be that much worse off
than you are now. On the other hand if you do not take care of the child
the care of it would fall upon the State, thus adding to the very heavy
burden it is already carrying. Therefore, I think that we, in behalf of the
State, should have a little something to say about this. From long years
of experience and record we know that children of defective parents are
almost sure to be defective themselves, and there is no question that Evelyn

is not a mental defective, and it is very probable that any child that she might have would be a defective also. I have been called to examine three girls during the last three years of a much higher grade mentality than is Evelyn. I made up my mind that these girls were mental defectives, and I told the people in charge of them the dangers just as I am telling you and advised them to place the girls in an institution that they might be taken care of. My advice, however, was not followed, and all three of the girls are here in the institution now after having had an illegitimate child.

I cannot believe that you would knowingly take any steps that would subject Evelyn to a danger of this sort. I do no mean by this that Evelyn is to be considered a bad girl, but simply as I say that her judgment and self-control is almost entirely lacking, and what she might do would be done through ignorance, and not through any evil intention.

There is another thing to be considered. I am convinced that the city of Newport has quite as many cases of this sort of girl as they desire, and that they have taken steps to have several of them properly cared for lately. It is quite possible that should you persist in your intention to remove Evelyn from the institution that they might consider it their duty to interfere in some way. I am quite sure that you will find it to your advantage and to Evelyn's advantage in the long run to allow her to stay here at least for several years longer.

Very truly yours,
Dr. Joseph H. Ladd, Supt.

February 26, 1916

My dear Mrs. Cook:-

I beg to acknowledge receipt of your note of the 23rd inquiring for your children. In reply permit me to say that they are all in good health and getting along very nicely. I would say that the boys are not attending school, but they will attend as soon as our school is open, which we expect to be in about two weeks. We had planned to open our school in September last year, but owing to delays in installation of our heating plant and other necessary equipment it has been impossible to open it up to this time.

There has been no change so far as the necessity for Evelyn's remaining in the institution is concerned. I believe I told you in a previous letter that she should be allowed to remain here at least as long as she is capable of bearing children. Evelyn's mental condition is not one of insanity, which can be cured, but one of mental defect, which is incurable, and which unfits Evelyn for properly adapting herself to conditions out in the world, and she should not be put out on her own responsibility.

Very truly yours,
Joseph H. Ladd, Supt.

June 5, 1916

My dear Miss Thomas:-

I wonder if I would be possible to have Evelyn Cook committed here by the court. Her mother comes up every little while, and has a good deal to say about taking her home, and I am afraid sometime she will be able to get Evelyn away, and we shall lose control of her. I consider Evelyn, while she is a good worker, would be an extremely dangerous character to have in the community.

I should imagine that it might be possible, considering Evelyn's personal history and her family history, to convince Judge Baker that she is a suitable case to be legally restrained.

Evelyn is talking about a vacation now, and I think her mother will try to get her out of the School at the earliest possible moment.

Very truly yours,
Joseph H. Ladd, Supt.

June 9, 1916

My dear Dr. Ladd:

As Miss Thomas is away on a three months vacation, and is not expected
in Newport until July, I am answering your letter of June 5th in regard
to having Evelyn Cook committed to your school by the court. I have
communicated with two physicians who will be very glad to see Evelyn and
testify as to her condition. Judge Baker says he will do all that is possible to
have her legally restrained.

   Of course it will be necessary to bring Evelyn to Newport. Would it be
possible or you to send her as far as Wickford? I will meet her there and
bring her to Newport. As I expect to be very busy the early part of next
week, the latter part, possibly Thursday, would be most convenient for
me. If this day would be satisfactory for you kindly let me know as soon
as possible and I shall make arrangements with the physicians. If it will be
impossible for you to send Evelyn to Wickford, I will arrange to come to
Exeter for her, in which case it will probably be necessary for her to remain
in Newport over night.

Sincerely yours,
Emily Carroll
Acting Secretary, Charity Organization Society

July 26, 1916

To Dr Ladd

Dear sir,

I wish to ask you if you will be kind enough to let Evelyn come home for a
vacation for two weeks. I would very much like to have her for the Fourth
of July. I hope the two boys are well and getting along nicely. I am glad that
you received the things I sent for Evelyn and that they were all useful for
her. I will be responsible for her while she will be at home and also on the
train and boat.

Sincerely yours,
Mrs. Loretta Cook

June 29, 1916

My dear Mrs. Cook:-

I beg to acknowledge receipt of your note of June 26th concerning Evelyn's vacation. In reply permit me to say that I do not consider it wise for Evelyn to go home for a vacation. She has been getting along quite nicely for a long time now, and I do not feel like running the risk of having this good behavior broken up.

  Following her previous vacation she was very impudent and saucy for a long time and made herself extremely disagreeable.

Very truly yours,
Joseph H. Ladd, Supt.

September 15, 1916

To Dr. Ladd

Dear sir,

I write to you requesting that you would be so kind as to inform me of my daughter Evelyn's condition, as I am very anxious to have her with me.

As I should think by this time she should be able to be of some service and company to me, I would like to hear from you concerning this as soon as possible. As I am now situated where I can make her perfectly comfortable and at the same time she can be of service to me as my time is taken up all the time. Kindly give this matter your consideration and oblige.

Yours respectfully,
Mrs. Loretta Cook

September 16, 1916

My dear Mrs. Cook:-

I beg to acknowledge receipt of your letter of inquiry concerning Evelyn. In reply I am glad to tell you that she is in excellent physical condition, and in the same condition as usual mentally.

  As I have written you before I do not consider Evelyn a proper person to have loose in a community, and I do not see my way clear to discharge her, and as you very well know I am not alone in my opinion concerning Evelyn. Several of the people in Newport who are interested in the good of the community agree with me in this matter.

Very truly yours,
Joseph H. Ladd, Supt.

January 6, 1917

To Dr. Ladd

Dear sir,

I think it a duty as a mother to write these few lines to you to ask you what is the matter with Evelyn.

I feel very anxious over her as I have not had a letter from her in six weeks. I hope she is not sick or what reason has she in not being let to write.

You know Dr. Ladd that though the children are away from me that my heart and mind are with them. I am the only one they have to look to as a mother. You will be doing me a great kindness by letting me know.

I hope that Evelyn is improving and that she will be alright after a while.

I am glad that you received the children's packages and hope that they liked them

I am very glad Timothy goes to school and I hope he is getting along nicely in his learning. I wish you would be kind enough to let William go too. I hope they are good boys and that they are both well.

Yours respectfully,
Mrs. L Cook

January 8, 1917

My dear Mrs. Cook:-

The reason Evelyn has not written is because we thought it was best for the girls not to write home just now as we had a few cases of diphtheria. Evelyn is all right, she is perfectly well, and will probably be able to write in a week or two.

Very truly yours,
Joseph H. Ladd, Supt.

April 2, 1917

To Dr. Ladd

Dear sir,

I am writing you these few lines as mother of Evelyn to do me a great
kindness.

I would like to ask you how long it would be before you would be willing
to let Evelyn home. She has been in your charge for two years and three
months, and where I was advised to put her there it was the understanding
it was for one year.

Now Dr. Ladd don't you think in those two years she has a chance to
change from her wayward ways and improve? Would you not be willing
to give her a chance on probation for a month to see how she does? If we
don't get a show how do we know whether we will be better or not?

I have a home of my own and will promise you faithfully as her mother to
take good care of her.

You know Dr. Ladd she works in the laundry in the Home and I feel that
she would be able to help me in my own home to work. They did not tell
me when I put her there she would have to stay all this time. The lady said
I could have her home after the year was up.

I hope the boys are both well and glad they are going to school.

Sincerely,
Mrs. L Cook

April 3, 1917

My dear Mrs. Cook:-

I beg to acknowledge receipt of your note of April 2nd. It certainly is
unfortunate, and I cannot but sympathize with you on account of Evelyn,
but I am bound to say that Evelyn's condition is such that to preclude
the possibility of recovery, and I am fully convinced that Evelyn has not
changed to such a degree that she would be able to go home and live the
proper kind of life.

I am glad to say, however, that both the boys are in good condition, and
are getting along very nicely. They are not going to school at present, and
the teacher was obliged to leave on account of ill health, and we have not
yet secured one to take her place. However, as soon as we secure a teacher
the boys will return to school.

Very truly yours,
Joseph H. Ladd, Supt.

July 26, 1917

To Dr. Ladd

Dear sir,

I write these few lines to ask you a kindness, if you would be kind enough
to let Evelyn home for a vacation as she has not been home for two years
and I think it will be change for her. And her sister Marjorie is home and
I would like them to see one another. Glad the boys are getting along so
well. I will see that she will be alright same as before. So I hope you will be
willing to grant me this favor. Thanking you for your kindness in the past,

Sincerely yours,
Mrs. Loretta Cook

July 31, 1917

My dear Mrs. Cook:-

Concerning Evelyn's vacation I beg to say that I am held responsible by the
State authorities for Evelyn's well being and I do not feel that I can be held
responsible for Evelyn's conduct while she is out of the institution. For this
reason I am afraid that I shall have to refuse to allow her to go home on a
vacation.

Very truly yours,
Joseph H. Ladd, Supt.

Undated

Dear Doctor Ladd,

I wish to ask you if you will be kind enough to let my sister Miss Evelyn
Cook home on a vacation for a week as I want to see her and my dear
brother very bad.

I will remain as ever, very truly yours,
Marjorie Cook

April 25, 1918

My dear Dr. Ladd:-

I trust you will recall meeting me some three years ago at the State House in Providence when I was making arrangements about Earl Goodwin?

  You have a girl from my parish at your institution, Evelyn Cook. Her mother keeps wondering if she is well enough to come home. Would you be kind enough to write me frankly about the advisability of this girl coming home and I know I can definitely satisfy the other to act on your judgment.

  I only came to this parish last October so consequently I have never seen Evelyn, and I know nothing of her case. I do feel, however, that if you tell me that she ought to remain where she is that the mother will abide by your decision.

Very cordially yours,
Reverend C.W. Forster

April 29, 1918

My dear Mr. Forster:-

I beg to acknowledge receipt of your note of April 25th concerning Evelyn Cook. In reply permit me to say that there is no inmate in the institution of the necessity of whose remaining in the institution I am more convinced than in the case of Evelyn Cook.

Evelyn is a decided mental defective, and the whole family seems to be in the same condition, and I feel just as sure that Evelyn would get into trouble if out in the world as I feel the sun will rise each morning. Evelyn is just the type of girl that fills our houses of ill fame, and I certainly never should advocate her leaving the institution.

Very truly yours,
Joseph H. Ladd, Supt.

November 1, 1918

My dear Mrs. Cook:-

I am sorry to tell you that Evelyn has the influenza. If she becomes
seriously ill I will notify you at once.

Very truly yours,
Joseph H. Ladd, Supt.

January 22, 1919

My dear Miss Emery:-

I suppose you are acquainted with Mrs. Loretta Cook, and probably you
know that we have three of her children here at the institution.

 During the course of conversation with Mrs. Cook she told me she
has another daughter at home who absolutely refused to obey her and
frequently runs away in the evening and spends the evenings out with
young fellows and girls. Of course there is no better place for a young
person to spend their time than in company with young people of the right
sort, but I fear that the sort of company that a disobedient, impudent girl
would likely seek would not be the right sort. To my mind this girl ought to
be looked after before things go too far, and while possibly it is out of your
jurisdiction I thought it would do no harm to speak about it. I suggested
to Mrs. Cook she better send the girl here. From observation of Mrs. Cook
and from the fact that three of her children are here undoubtedly feeble-
minded it is evident that the other girl, Marjorie, is also feeble-minded and
should be cared for before serious results occur. There is also another child
in the Children's Home that in my opinion is also mentally defective and
should be sent to an institution while he is still young.

 If we can get control of all these children then we have put a sure stop to
the continuation of that family.

Very truly yours,
Joseph H. Ladd, Supt.

May 9, 1919

Dear Dr. Ladd:-

I have been consulted by Mrs. Loretta Cook, mother of Evelyn Cook, who is now an inmate of your School, and has been such for the past four years. Miss Cook was sent to your School when she was fifteen years of age because of being a little wild and somewhat incorrigible. She has repeatedly written her mother and asked her to secure her release. I would appreciate it very much, Doctor, in behalf of Mrs. Cook, whom I have known for a long time, if you could see your way clear to parole Evelyn. Of course, my request is based upon the statement of the other that she feels that Evelyn is fully capable now, under the mother's care and guidance, to look out for her and care for herself. I wish to thank you in advance, in behalf of Mrs. Cook, for any interest which you may take in this matter.

Yours truly,
M. Sully
Attorney at Law

May 9, 1919

Dear Miss Cook:-

Your mother has consulted me with reference to the contents of your letter
to her of May 4th, and you may rest assured that I am doing everything
in my power to secure your parole from the Home. I trust that you will
continue to keep up your good behavior and conduct so that you will make
it as easy as possible for us to secure your release. Your mother is doing
everything possible for you and we both hope that in the very near future,
your condition permitting, you will be able to return to your home and
mother. I am this day writing to Dr. Ladd in your behalf.

Yours very truly,
M. Sully
Attorney at Law

May 19, 1919

My dear Mr. Sully,

I beg to acknowledge receipt of your note concerning Evelyn Cook. In reply I would say that the proper course for you to pursue is to make an application for Evelyn's parole to the Penal and Charitable Commission at the State House.

In connection with this case I beg to say that Mrs. Cook has tried many times before to have Evelyn discharged from the institution and I always have discouraged her, and I am afraid that I cannot honestly change my attitude in this case now. I am convinced in my own mind that Evelyn is the type of girl who is bound to go wrong sexually if she has a ghost of a chance to exhibit any tendencies of this sort, and yet we find that she is very prone to be mixed up in anything of the sort that does occur. However, the Penal and Charitable Commission have authority to discharge Evelyn if they see fit to do so, or to direct me to allow her to go on parole. Personally I think it is a mistake to consider the discharge of girls of her type, and especially at this time when the Government is trying its best to lessen the number of prostitutes and venereal infection.

I beg to say that I took the liberty of intercepting the letter which you sent to Evelyn, as I did not consider it wise to allow any false hopes in her. I believe when authority for her discharge has been obtained from the proper source will be time enough to talk to Evelyn about going home. I trust that you will not consider that I have overstepped my rights in the matter of withholding this letter.

Very truly yours,
Joseph H. Ladd, Supt.

May 22, 1919

Gentlemen:-

I have received from a Mr. Sully, Attorney at Law, of Newport application for the release of Evelyn Cook. She has been committed to the institution by the court.

  To my mind this is a case that should receive very careful consideration before the girl is discharged. I am very positive from having seen and talked with Mrs. Cook, the mother, that she is more or less mentally deficient herself, and is the mother of five mentally deficient children. This is an undoubted case of hereditary transmission with every great probability that any child that Evelyn might have would be feeble-minded. I am sure this is a case, if ever there was one, that should be held in the institution during the child-bearing period. If it is deemed wise to discharge her before this period is naturally terminated then it should be artificially terminated before her discharge. At present there is no law in Rhode Island permitting this artificial termination. Therefore, my recommendation is that this girl be allowed to remain in the institution until she is past this period.

  I might say that we have three of Mrs. Cook's children in the institution at the present time, and there are two more in Newport. One of these a girl, a little younger than Evelyn, is living at home with the mother and the mother tells me she is absolutely uncontrollable.

  My idea in recommending the retention of these girls in the institution is not that by so doing prostitution may be suppressed or lessened in any appreciable degree, but rather that the State in the future may be relieved of the support of the feeble-minded children that are likely to come from these girls, if things are allowed to take their natural course.

  When these girls become prostitutes they are very likely to become the lowest of the type and become more than ordinarily dangerous from the standpoint of the spread of venereal infection, due to the fact that they lack initiative and are very careless, and take no steps to care for themselves in connection with these infections. While these girls are not infected at the present time, and nobody can state with absolute certainty that they ever would be yet it seems to me that at this time when the Government is endeavoring to do everything possible to prevent infection of the retuning soldiers, it is an inopportune time for the discharge of these girls.

Very truly yours,
Joseph H. Ladd, Supt.

June 5, 1919

My dear Mrs. Cook:-

Enclosed you will find the latest letter which you sent to Evelyn. As I think I have told you several times before it is not treating Evelyn properly to send her such a letter as this. It only tends to make her very discontented and unhappy.

It is your privilege to go ahead and take whatever steps you deem advisable to secure Evelyn's discharge from the institution, but do not write her all about it, and it is a bad thing for you to tell Evelyn of your very poor opinion of the people who differ from you on the question of Evelyn's discharge. It tends to make her resentful toward all of us and in this way makes her disobedient and unruly and gets her into difficulties.

It is of no use for you to waste your time and postage in sending such letters to her for I shall not deliver them. I shall be very glad indeed to give her any letter which you may send which is of a pleasant, agreeable tone, but I refuse to give her any letter that I think is intended to irritate her and make her discontented.

Very truly yours,
Joseph H. Ladd, Supt.

June 23, 1919

To Dr. Ladd

Dear sir,

I now write these few lines to ask you if anything is wrong with Evelyn or William as I have not heard from them in five or six weeks. I hope you are not punishing them with what I had to say. You know that I have a mother's feeling for my children and you cannot blame me for liking to have them with me. But as I understand you are the one that is in the position to say what you think is right. You know Evelyn is there four years last January and the boys will be four in September. And Evelyn said you had let others out on trial for a month or two to see how they behave and why not her? How can you tell when you don't give her a chance? She must be improved in four years. How do you think William and Timothy are getting along and how long have they got to stay? Hoping if I have not said anything that you will allow Evelyn to write to me as I feel very anxious when I don't hear from them.

Oblige,
Yours truly,
Mrs. L Cook

August 5, 1919

To Dr. Ladd

Dear Sir,

I think it my duty to write you a few lines. I was very pleased the way I
found the boys and Evelyn on Saturday. Mrs. M, the matron, told me that
Evelyn had a very good record and she was very pleased with everything
she was doing. So I wish it will not be too much to ask if you will let Evelyn
home as soon as you can as I have a nice place for her as I need her help.
I know from my heart that she will do as I want her as she has learned a
lesson in four years and a half. For she promised me she would do right
and she knows what it will mean both to you and me.

   Hoping you will let her home as soon as possible. The boys look very
good. Timothy has grown and so has William. Do you think you will send
William to school so he can learn to read and write?

Yours sincerely,
Mrs. Loretta Cook

August 24, 1919

To Dr. Ladd

Dear sir,

I write these few lines to ask you a kindness. As long as you promised me
you would let Evelyn home, I wish you would let her home to me by Labor
Day which is a week from Monday if you could as I would be pleased to
have her before the season closes. Hoping you grant my request.

Yours truly,
Mrs. Loretta Cook

September 2, 1919

Gentlemen:

I would recommend that Evelyn Cook be allowed to go home on parole. Her mother is very anxious to have her come and says she has a good place for her to work.

  The girl herself has been doing very well indeed for some time now and I feel that she ought to have a chance to make good.

Very truly yours,
Joseph H. Ladd, Supt.

September 11, 1919

My dear Miss Emery:

Evelyn Cook, one of our girls in whom I believe you are interested, has
been doing so well for some time that we have decided to allow her to go
home on probation. I should esteem it a favor if you could find time to
look Evelyn up once in a while and see how she gets along. I told Mrs.
Cook that I should ask you to do this and that I should expect her to look
out for Evelyn.

  Thanking you in advance for anything that you may be able to do for
Evelyn, I remain

Very sincerely yours,
Joseph H. Ladd, Supt.

September 11, 1919

My dear Mrs. Cook:

I beg to inform you that the Penal and Charitable Commission have voted to allow Evelyn to go home on parole. I told you at the time I talked with you about Evelyn going home that I should ask Miss Emery to try and have a little over sight of Evelyn. From some things that you have said to me, I am led to believe that you do not have the most kindly feeling in the world toward Miss Emery. If this is the case, I shall expect you not to show any ill feeling toward Miss Emery if she has occasion to speak to you in regard to Evelyn. I trust there will be no occasion for this and that Evelyn will do as well as she promised to do and doubtless intends to do.

Very truly yours,
Joseph H. Ladd, Supt.

November 17, 1919

My dear Dr. Ladd:-

In answer to your letter, Evelyn was going out with a particular sailor but he is home now for several weeks and so there is no chance of her being with him for the present. I have told Mrs. Cook that she must keep Evelyn away from the boys.

  Personally I do not think Evelyn should be out on parole as I do not feel that Mrs. Cook has enough influence over her.

Very truly yours,
Helen M. Emery
Protective Officer

February 11, 1920

My dear Dr. Ladd:-

I have heard that Mrs. Cook intends to make an effort to have Evelyn released from Exeter.

   Evelyn has been working as a waitress for Mrs. Curley until very recently when she left saying she was going to be married. Mrs. Curley thinking she made up this story for an excuse to leave, as she was getting another maid, did not notify me. Last Saturday Reverend Mr. Forster, rector of Emmanuel Church reported to me that he had heard that Evelyn had taken out a marriage license. Later he telephoned me that Evelyn and William Edward Solomon, yoe., Yardcraft Office, Training Station, had come to him to be married – both were under age and both had their parents consent. Mr. Forster said his conscience would not allow him to marry them. Evelyn was held and returned to Exeter as you know. Mr. Solomon came to see me and stated that he had been going with the girl again ever since he returned from his furlough which was just after Thanksgiving. That he has been to her house a number of times and that Mrs. Cook was sometimes in the downstair tenement where she was taking care of a sick woman. He acknowledged having had intercourse with the girl and although he had been told she was feeble-minded he was willing to marry her and "take a chance."

Very truly yours,
Helen Emery
Probation Officer

February 16, 1920

My dear Mr. Blackmar:-

Evelyn Cook, concerning whom I telephoned, was placed in Exeter
January 1915 at the request of her mother and through the interest of
Dr. Potter, Emmanuel Church. It was found necessary to put her under
restraint at that time as she was utterly unmanageable at home and on
the streets with boys. Her mother was so persistent in her efforts to have
the girl released and Dr. Ladd felt so strongly that it would be unwise to
release her that on June 15, 1916 she was sent to Newport that she might
be committed through the Court on the testimony of Drs. McGuire and
McLeod.

  She remained at the school until September 1919 when Dr. Ladd decided
to release her on parole in my care. Although she has been working during
almost all this time she has had three different places. At the last she was
fairly satisfactory but had been reprimanded twice for having a young
sailor, William Edward Solomon (20 yrs) at the house. As early as October
she was reported as being out late with the sailor which information was
given at that time to Dr. Ladd. The girl and her mother were interviewed
and sailor was told that she had been at Exeter and promised not to see
her again. As the mother seemed to have little influence over the girl it was
a question at that time whether it would not be necessary to return her to
Exeter. As she still continued to hold her position and was well liked and
as she had promised not to see the sailor again and he had left from town
on leave she was given another chance. The mother promised to report if
anything went wrong and the girl herself reported occasionally and was
visited.

  During a month's absence of the Probation Officer from the office, in
which no report came from the mother, the girl left her work and obtained

a marriage license signed by her mother to marry the sailor. February
8th, Revered Mr. Forster, Emmanuel Church, reported that the couple
were there to be married and that he did not feel his conscience would
allow him to perform the ceremony. The sailor had obtained his mother's
consent not knowing facts of the case. No amount of persuasion could
convince him that the girl was feeble-minded or if she was he had no right
to marry her. After interviews with Mr. Forster, probation officer, Captain
Dismukes, Training Station, the boy still remained unconvinced.
Meanwhile the girl was taken charge of and held overnight until she could
be taken to Exeter the following morning. The boy acknowledged that he
has had intercourse with the girl on various occasions and that he believed
her pregnant but that he had gotten out the license before he knew this
and that was not the reason he felt he must marry her. He immediately
appealed to his superior officers - quoted the case of a boy who had eloped
with a girl from a school for the feeble-minded - married her and fought
the case in the New York Courts and kept her from recommitment.
The mother has sought legal advice and has gone about with a petition
for the girl's release which she has asked the girl's employer and different
friends to sign. She met Mr. Forster in front of the church on Sunday
morning and invoked curses saying that she had prayed he be struck dead
as he entered the pulpit for giving me "the tip." The sailor, I understand, is
to be placed on "general detail" and as soon as possible transferred.
Evelyn has a sister, Marjorie, recently committed to Exeter and has two
brothers, Timothy and William also at the school. The younger brother,
Robert, at the Children's Home in this city, showing the same tendency is
in line for Exeter while the mother, Mrs. Loretta Cook has demonstrated
her mentality.

   Dr. Ladd considers them a second Kallikak family.

Very truly yours,
Helen Emery, Probation Officer

March 3, 1920

Dear Sir:

I write you in behalf of Mrs. Loretta Cook, the mother of Miss Evelyn
Cook, now confined in your school. Mrs. Cook informs me that she has
not heard from her daughter since the latter's recent confinement, a period
of about a month, although she, herself has written to her daughter.

  Mrs. Cook is somewhat worried in not hearing from her daughter, so
I am writing you to ask if you will inform me if you are able whether or
not Miss Cook is sick and why if she is not sick she has neglected to write
home.

  I trust that you will appreciate the anxiety that this is causing Mrs. Cook
and will favor me with a prompt reply.

Very truly yours,
Frank Nolan
Counselor at Law

March 4, 1920

My dear Mr. Nolan:

I beg to acknowledge receipt of your note of March 3rd. In reply, I am
very glad to inform you that the Cook children are all in most excellent
health. The reason that Mrs. Cook does not hear from her children is
that they do not write when they have an opportunity, or that they write
letters of such a nature that it does not seem wise to send them. Mrs. Cook
herself insists on writing letters tending to make her children unhappy
and discontented in the institution. I have written her time and time again
trying to make her understand that it is an unkindness to write such letters
to her children. The children are of such dispositions that they would be
quite contented and happy if she would let them alone, but practically all
of her letters contain references to their being taken out, suggestions that
they are terribly abused and such things as that. I have told Mrs. Cook that
I shall not give these letters to the children because it is not good for them.
I do not know how much Mrs. Cook has told you about her daughters, but
I will say that in practically every letter that the girls write are statements
tending to sustain unfortunate connections with Newport and I do not
consider it wise to keep those connections alive. If you can explain to Mrs.
Cook in a way that she will understand that she is not doing a kindness to
her children in writing these pitying letters to them, you certainly will be
doing a great kindness to her children and herself as well. As I said, I have
tried to explain this to her several times but evidently I have been unable
to convey the idea.

Very truly yours,
Joseph H. Ladd ,Supt.

March 4, 1920

To Dr. Joseph Ladd

Dear Sir:-

Mrs. Cook, the mother of Marjorie and Evelyn, is very anxious to know something in regard to Evelyn's health. Would you kindly ask Evelyn to write to her mother, or if that is not possible, write us in regard to her.

Sincerely yours,
Helen Emery
Probation Officer

March 24, 1920

Dear Sir:

Probably you never thought that you would hear from me and again you may have been waiting for this letter. That I do not know. I have decided to write to you on a very important matter which is more important to me than the money which I earn every day. It has to do with my very being which you will later find out through the course of this letter. It is the being of Evelyn Cook, the girl who was to be my wife and who was taken away from me on the very day of our wedding because she is said to be feeble-minded. I do not know whether this be true or not. In fact I do not believe it to be true.

Now, I am going to put a proposition before you which I want you to give due consideration. It is this, you believe Evelyn to be in trouble. If she is then I consider it my duty, as a man who carried an honorable name from a father already dead thirteen years, to marry this girl and give her a home and still hold fast to the name of Solomon. I am willing that you should operate upon her after the birth of the child so that she will not be able to bear any more children if you will let me marry her before the birth of the child. Not only marry her but have her. I give you my word of honor to do what is right by the girl if you will only give her to me. I will give her a home and the best of surroundings. If you wish you may show this letter to Evelyn. I am sure that she will agree with me. You see I do not do this behind anyone's back. My mother and Evelyn's mother both know of this move. I also ask your permission to come and visit Evelyn at the school and to have a personal interview with you any week either Saturday or Sunday.

Yours Truly,
William Solomon
U.S.S. Chas. AUSBURN, Navy Yard Boston

March 30, 1920

Dear Sir:

I beg to acknowledge receipt of your note of March 27th. It is useless to go
into any discussion of the ethics of this cause, but the point is this. From
all appearances Evelyn Cook is a member of a mentally defective family.
The mental defect extends back at least three generations. Evelyn herself
is a mental defective and so far as we can determine, all her brothers and
sisters are the same. With a family history of this sort, it is very likely that
any children that Evelyn might have will be mental defectives. We do
not consider the perpetuation of a strain of this sort to be wise, from any
standpoint. For this reason, I shall do all that lies in my power to prevent
you having any further communication with the girl. As for your coming
to see her, no good could be achieved by that I should refuse to allow you
to see her if you came. The best thing that you can do for the girl as well as
for yourself, is to forget that you ever saw her.

Very truly yours,
Joseph H. Ladd, Supt.

March 23, 1921

Dr. Ladd

Dear sir:

I now write these few lines to you as I would like to know if you would please do me a kind favor.

   I am very sorry that I made the mistake I did after you being so kind to let me out before. I have thought things over and seen my mistake, and know by this time I have learned a good lesson, and could honestly say if you would please give me one more chance I will take good care of myself and my baby and be a help to my mother.

Hoping to hear from you soon.

Yours truly,
Miss Evelyn Cook

April 5, 1921

My dear Evelyn:-

Your note of recent date is received, and in reply permit me to say that
we can do nothing about your going away until you have returned to the
school.

I trust you are well and getting along nicely.

Very truly yours,
Joseph H. Ladd, Supt.

April 20, 1921

Dear Dr. Ladd:-

Mrs. Cook is getting anxious about Evelyn. I tried to explain that Evelyn
needs special protection, and that her confinement is not a question of
punishment for wrong doing. I think it would be more satisfactory if you
would report directly to Mrs. Cook, and emphasis the need of oversight
because of Evelyn's weakness. I told her that I would ask you to write to
her.

  Thanking you for your co-operation, I am,

Very sincerely,
Helen Emery
Protective Officer

May 5, 1921

My dear Miss Emery:-

I beg to acknowledge receipt of your note of April 20th concerning Mrs.
Cook and Evelyn.

I shall be glad to write the letter to Mrs. Cook which you suggest, but I
feel quite confident that it will fail to penetrate. You are well aware to Mrs.
Cook's mental condition, and I have found that my talk to her has about
as much effect upon her as water upon a duck's back.

However, I will write to her.

Very truly yours,
Joseph H. Ladd, Supt.

May 5, 1921

My dear Mrs. Cook:-

A few days ago I received from Miss Emery a letter stating that you were
a good deal disturbed because you felt that Evelyn was confined in an
institution as a punishment for things that she has done. Miss Emery asked
me to write to you in regard to this matter.

  I wish to say that Evelyn is not confined as a punishment for anything
that she has done, but on account of her mental condition. Evelyn is not
a normal girl mentally and is not equipped to take care of herself in a
community. There is great probability also that any children that she would
have would be more or less abnormal mentally, and also it is probably that
she would have a good many of these children if she were outside. It is for
these reasons that it seems best for her to remain in this institution.

Very truly yours,
Joseph H. Ladd, Supt.

May 10, 1921

My dear Miss Emery:-

Enclosed you will find the letter from Mrs. Cook to me in response to my
letter endeavoring to explain why Evelyn was detained at the institution.

  I thought you might be interested to see Mrs. Cook's reaction to my
efforts. I might say that I have always obtained similar results to any effort
to explain this to Mrs. Cook.

Very truly yours,
Joseph H. Ladd ,Supt.

May 14, 1921

My dear Dr. Ladd:-

I am in receipt of your letter of the 11th with letter from Mrs. Cook. I am not at all surprised at the contents of her letter, but I could not refuse her request, as she wanted a report in regard to Evelyn, and for that reason I wrote you. I had no hope that she would understand, and any effort made by anyone interested in the family here to make her understand would be absolutely useless. I have always insisted that as you are in charge, you were the one best able to judge what was best for the children. I have, of course, told her flatly that Evelyn was not like other girls and for that reason she was confined.

Thanking you for your patience in the matter, I am,

Very sincerely,
Helen Emery
Protective Officer

June 9, 1921

To Dr Ladd

Dear Sir

I received your letter some time ago and was very glad to hear from you.

Why don't you think I am able to go out?

I explained to you when I wrote before that you would be able to trust me as I have learned a good lesson. I hope you don't think I cannot be trusted as I don't care for him any more. He is far away and I never even think about him. I intend to do as you want me to. I hope you will give me another chance so I can show you that I will do right without returning to the school.

I am getting along nicely.

Hoping to hear from you soon.

Respectfully yours,
Evelyn Cook

June 16, 1921

My dear Evelyn:-

I beg to acknowledge receipt of your note of June 9th. It hardly seems
desirable for us to discuss this matter mentioned in your letter as we
should not get anywhere by doing so.

I am glad to know however that you are getting along so well at Howard. I
hope you will continue to get along well.

Very truly yours,
Joseph H. Ladd, Supt.

October 10, 1921

Dear Dr. Ladd:

Your letter received the other day, and in reference to the attitude of
certain of your charges left here, I would say that your friend, Annie
Allison is pugnacious and combative, the same as ever, and has a very
strong forceful way of expressing her sentiments.

  Also a former inmate of yours, transferred here, Evelyn Cook by name,
left us rather suddenly Saturday night with her child, and you may perhaps
hear of her doings through the Newport Society. On account of the tearing
down of buildings and destruction of fences about the institution, there
is a very open place about this time, and we expect others will wander out
into the world to seek their fortunes again.

With my kindest regards,
Henry Jones, M.D., Supt., State Infirmary

October 14, 1921

My dear Dr. Jones:-

I received quite a shock when I got your letter of October 10th. I sincerely hope that we shall be able to get track of Evelyn, and have her returned to our institution, as I am very sure she is not the type of girl to be at large.

Very truly yours,
Joseph H. Ladd, Supt.

February 3, 1922

My dear Dr. Ladd,

For some time we have tried to learn the whereabouts of Evelyn Cook but
without success. We visited Mrs. Loretta Cook's home, but could find
no trace of her. Mrs. Cook was not at home at the time of the visit and a
neighbor said that she lived all alone.

  We have been in touch with Mrs. Cook during the winter as she
frequently asks us to help her in finding day's work. One lady for whom
she is working telephoned this office this week to ask if we knew what
had happened to Loretta Cook as she had not come to work on her
regular day (Tuesday) and had not sent word that she was not coming. The
woman said that Mrs. Cook went to Providence every weekend and had
telephoned from Providence once saying that she would not be back for
her work on Tuesday. This woman has just telephoned again and said that
Loretta was still in Providence but would be back for work next Tuesday.
We will try to get some definite information as to where Loretta Cook
goes in Providence as we are inclined to believe that Evelyn is probably
living there and she is visiting Evelyn every week end. If we learn anything
definite we shall notify you.

Sincerely yours,
Harriet Thomas
Secretary, Charity Organization Society

February 7, 1922

My dear Miss Thomas:-

In reply to your note of February 3rd I beg to say that I should be glad to know exactly Evelyn's whereabouts.

I have not made up my mind yet whether it is quite worthwhile going after Evelyn or not, but I should like to know where she is so I could go and get her if I decided to.

Personally I think she should be brought back to the institution and kept here during the rest of her reproductive life at least. However, if we go and get her while she is apparently doing well her mother will stir up all the unpleasantness she can about it, and to my mind it is more or less a question which is the more desirable course to pursue.

Very truly yours,
Joseph H. Ladd, Supt.

March 10, 1922

Gentlemen:-

There is a movement on foot to secure the parole of Evelyn Cook to the
custody of her mother. I wish to present my opinions in regard to this
matter for the consideration of the Commission.

Evelyn Cook was admitted to this school January 12, 1915, and improved
very markedly. After repeated solicitation by the mother I consented to
allow Evelyn to go on parole in September 1919, the mother promising
faithfully to look after her, to see that she as properly employed and
that she had no opportunity to associate with the men. The mother also
promised to allow Miss Emery to help with the supervision of Evelyn. The
mother reported to me several times that Evelyn was employed in proper
occupation, and was doing well.

After Evelyn had been on parole several months Miss Emery found
she had been out with a young man until two o'clock in the morning.
This young man, a naval man, was soon transferred to another base. The
mother continued to report that everything was well with Evelyn. Then
Miss Emery discovered that Evelyn was engaged to marry this young man,
who had returned to Newport. Upon discovering this Evelyn was returned
by Miss Emery to the institution.

We soon found that she was pregnant, and she was transferred to the
State Infirmary for confinement. Just before the time she was to be
returned to the school she escaped from the Infirmary with her child, and
we have as yet been unable to locate her.

In my estimation Evelyn Cook is a high grade mental defective, and her
mental defect is due to heredity. It has been found that a large majority of
children born of such a parent are mentally defective. I have three other
members of the same family in the school, one a girl who has shown

uncontrollable sexual impulses. It seems to me that this is a family that the State could better do without, and that the sooner and more certainly the propagation of this strain is stopped the better it will be.

Mr. Fletcher Loughton of Newport is very actively interesting himself in this case, solely on the grounds of the mother's loneliness. Certainly no-one can help sympathizing with the mother in her condition, but in view of the fact that she was unable to control either of her daughters when she had charge of them before they entered the school, and in view of the further tact that she did not properly control and care for Evelyn when she was paroled out to her before, I do not feel justified in recommending her parole again to the mother.

Respectfully submitted,
Joseph H. Ladd, Supt.

October 15, 1923

My dear Miss Thomas:

The last letter from the above mentioned girl that I can find in her sister, Marjorie's folder was written from Providence on May 26, 1923 and mailed from Boston on June 3. In it she speaks of spending Christmas and Easter at home. She also speaks about going to Franklin Park. This is in Boston.

She has written to the other children since but the letters have all gone through, as there was nothing undesirable in them.

We would be interested to learn if she is in Newport and if she is married. One of our discharged girls wrote to a present patient that Evelyn was married. Interesting!

Sincerely,
Miss Mary F. McTernan
Social Worker

March 15, 1924

My dear Dr. Ladd:-

The Boston family Welfare Society wrote to the Newport Family Welfare Society that Evelyn Cook was living at Worcester Street, Boston, with John Bell, to whom she said she was married. The marriage has not been verified. At present, the man is in the hospital. The Society is going to help Evelyn's four year old daughter, Ruth, in a day nursery, and is going to help the mother. They wrote to inquire if Evelyn's mother could assist her in any way.

  Miss Thomas gave us the above information, and asked us to forward it to you.

Very sincerely,
Helen Emery
Probation Officer

March 18, 1924

My dear Miss Wilcox:

I did not write to thank you for getting the information on the Cole case
but I am very grateful just the same for it. Application for the boy's transfer
to Massachusetts has been made.

Today Dr. Ladd forwarded me a copy of a letter sent him by the Probation
Officer in Newport in regard to the above mentioned patient. I will not see
the doctor until March 20 and so decided I would write you little bit on
the case.

We have her sister and two brothers as patients here. She was also a
patient for a long time. Finally, she was allowed to go home on trial to
her mother who is mentally below par. She was not out long till several
damaging reports came to the notice of the School and she was brought
back but found out pregnant. When the time came she was transferred to
our State Infirmary for confinement. She escaped from there. It has not
been possible to get hold of her since although it has been suspected that
she has been in Newport. The girl belongs in a School for Feebleminded
but we have no authority to go over into Massachusetts and take her.

If Dr. Ladd writes to you will you please send me a carbon copy of the
reply. This will do away with the need of replying directly to me. I think
you will remember that I told you I only see the doctor once a week in this
time of the year.

Sincerely,
Miss Mary F. McTernan
Social Worker

March 18, 1924

Dear Miss Thomas,

Many, many thanks for the summaries you sent us on the Thompson and
Rogers cases.

  Dr. Ladd has just forwarded me a copy of a letter that Miss Emery wrote
on Evelyn Cook. By a strange coincidence I met Mrs. Cook in Miss
Emery's office in March. I had not seen her before although I had visited
the house.

  Do you happen to know a Mr. Martin who is doing his best to get all the
others out for her? He ought to know about Evelyn and then judge how
wise it would be to let the others out.

Sincerely,
Mary F. McTernan
Social Worker

March 27, 1924

Gentlemen:-

I understand that you have under your care a young woman named Bell,
residing at Worcester Street. This young woman was formerly Evelyn Cook
of Newport, and is legally an inmate of our institution. She was transferred
to another institution for temporary care and escaped while there. We have
three members of the same family here; one a girl with an intelligence
quotient of 91, sexually immoral, one boy with an intelligence quotient of
57, and another boy with an intelligence quotient of 51.

   If you or the State of Massachusetts consider that all concerned would
be well served by having this young woman returned to our institution we
shall be willing to receive her at any time.

Very truly yours,
Joseph H. Ladd, Supt.

April 2, 1924

My dear Dr. Ladd:

Your letter of March 27 received regarding Evelyn Cook Bell. In regard
to her return to the Exeter School, it is very difficult for us to decide. If it
were not for the possibility of children, I should say without question to
let her remain as she is. She is happy and is employed at unskilled work
which apparently she can do in a fairly satisfactory manner. She is legally
married to a man who seems to be a decent sort of fellow and shares his
wife's devotion to the little girl, a sweet natured, attractive child who so far
(though of course she is only 3 years old) shows no indication of mental
defect.

Mr. Bell has just been discharged from the Homeopathic Hospital where
he was operated upon for Tubercular Epididemitis, and will probably be
able to go to work very soon.

Evelyn herself says she feels perfectly sure that she is not going to have any
children, but on what basis this conviction is made we have been unable to
discover. Possibly she is shrewd enough to realize that propagation on the
part of the feeble-minded is frowned upon, and feels that her chances of
being left at large in the community are better if she can convince people
that she will have no more children.

We are wondering whether there is anything in the record of Evelyn's
confinement at the State Infirmary that would indicate the possibility
of future sterility. We would be interested to know how Evelyn graded
mentally when she was at Exeter, and would greatly appreciate some
expression of opinion from you as to the possible or probable normality
of the children of a mother like Evelyn and a father who appears mentally
normal but has the above medical history.

We realize that we are giving you extremely little to judge from on the
paternal side, as Mr. Bell, who is a Greek, has no relatives in this country,

and we have no family history whatever. In any event, you are, of course, much better fitted to judge regarding the probable mentality of Evelyn's offspring than we can be.

Sincerely yours,
Florence Wilcox
Family Welfare Society of Boston

April 4, 1924

Further report on the Cook family, Newport, RI.

A visit was made at the Lenthal School, Newport, where Robert Cook is a fifth grade pupil. The teacher tells me he is a "queer acting child" but is doing more than average class work. She attributes this to the fact that he repeated the fourth grade. He is 11 years old.

The Boston Family Welfare Society wrote to the Newport agency in regard to Evelyn - who escaped from the Infirmary at Howard with her baby. On March 28 I verified the following information from the records of the Boston agency:

Evelyn was married June 15, 1922 to a Greek, John Bell. In the summer of 1922 they worked as chef and cook respectively at the New Hampshire State Hospital for Mental Diseases. They were discharged because of constant quarreling among themselves.

Evelyn has been aided on and off by the agency. Recently the man was in the hospital and Evelyn could not get work at all. The agency was aiding last week and apparently intended to aid, despite our recommend that this was a case that should be handled by a public agency and not use private funds to propagate inferior citizens. Dr. Ladd wrote telling the Society it could use its influence to have Evelyn returned to us.

Respectfully submitted,
Miss Mary F. McTernan
Social Worker

April 16, 1924

My dear Miss Wilcox:-

My attitude in the Bell case is entirely determined on general principals.
I think it is generally admitted that by far the greater number of desirable
citizens come from fairly good stock and from fairly good homes. By
fairly good homes I do not refer to the financial condition, but to the
intellectual, moral and emotional condition.

In the case of Mrs. Bell the heredity certainly is not good, and her
emotional reaction has not been good. There seems to be a strain of
emotional instability and defective mentality in her whole family. So from
the standpoint of both heredity and environment there seems to be quite
a question of the chances for success of any children that Mrs. Bell has or
may have.

I have no history concerning her confinement as this confinement
occurred in another institution, and from which she escaped before
time for her to return to us. I am writing to the Superintendent of the
Infirmary, however, for information concerning her confinement. When I
receive his reply I will notify you.

You understand that I am not arguing for the return of this girl to our
institution so long as Massachusetts desires to take care of her. We are
terribly overcrowded at present with many more cases on our waiting list.

Very truly yours,
Joseph H. Ladd, Supt.

April 16, 1924

My dear Dr. Jones:-

Evelyn Bell who was confined at your institution under the name of
Evelyn Cook assures the social agencies who have been obliged to furnish
pecuniary assistance to her that she is incapable of bearing more children.
Is there anything in the history of her confinement that would corroborate
this statement of hers.

Very truly yours,
Joseph H. Ladd, Supt.

April 21, 1924

Dear Dr. Ladd:

We find nothing in the history of Evelyn Cook alias Bell that would
prohibit her from bearing children.

Very truly yours,
Henry Jones, M.D., Supt., State Infirmary

July 26, 1926

Neighbor in mother's house thinks girl is "crazy," as nobody in right
mind would boast about being married, living with another man, getting
arrested, being put on probation, and then doing the same thing.

   Against mother's wishes Evelyn took Tommie to Boston a month ago.
Yesterday he wrote saying he had not worked in three weeks, and that
Evelyn's husband was in the White Mountains.

September 10, 1926

Letter carrier on route advises worker not to try to locate girl as owners
will not tell about tenants. He met Evelyn September 6 and she said she
was putting little girl in a home so she could have "more fun." He is not
surprised to learn where she was as he often thought she has escaped from
a "crazy house." She has had several affairs with Greeks and one got her
arrested. Matron at S. End Day Nursery often tempted to report cruelty of
Evelyn to SPCC.

February 25, 1927

At Dedham Street Boston, living with husband.

October 14, 1930

DISCHARGED

Mental Status: Moron
Total Duration of Institution Life: 15 years, 9 months, 2 days
Reason for Discharge: *Hasn't been heard from for years*

APPLICATION

by the Parents or Friends of Applicants for
School

ANSWER

R. Dunphy

1896

Rhode Island

Mother, Don't Let the Sun Set on You Here

The compulsory removal of a woman's reproductive organs was at once the ultimate solution to prohibiting the multiplication of the feeble-minded, and practically the only such measure not explicitly provided for by law.

State legislators did, in fact, debate the issue twice; and though many states passed compulsory sterilization laws for eugenic purposes in the 1920s and 30s, Rhode Island was not one of them. Instead, consistent with the doctrines handed down from the first generation of eugenicists at the oldest feeble-minded schools in the country, permanent custodial care was commonly enforced as a means of eradicating undesirable family bloodlines within the state's borders.

But Dr. Ladd's advocacy for sexual sterilization, which he voiced publicly as late as the 1940s, was not altogether unrequited. While hysterectomies and tubal ligations for birth control may not have been a common practice, some women - incorrigible cases with a history of illegitimate pregnancies - were coerced to undergo such operations in order to escape a life sentence in state custody at the feeble-minded school.

NOX VBES	ABSTRACT	JUDGEMENT		
		MORAL	CON-CRETE	

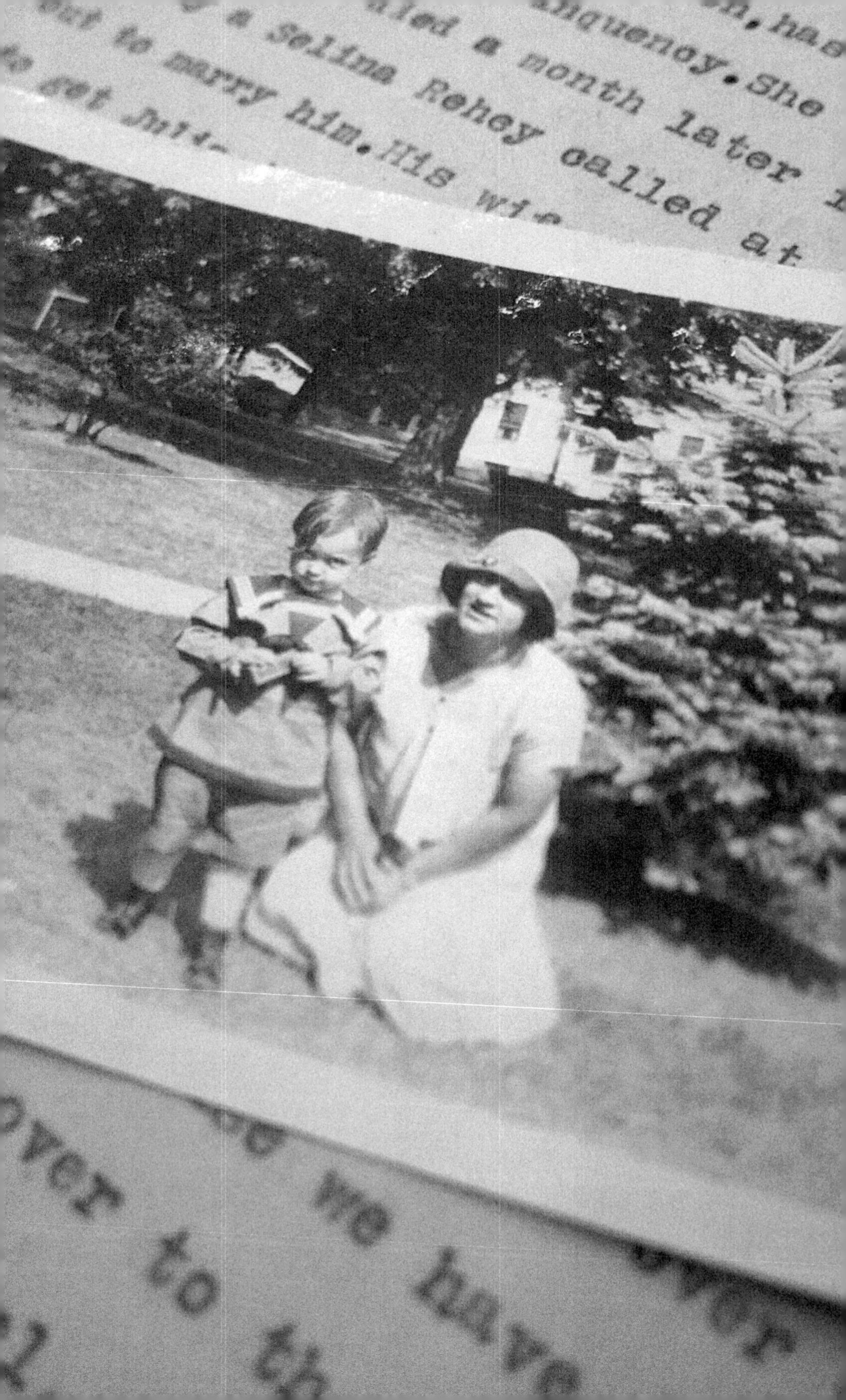

CORA

Cora Duffy. Twenty-eight years old. Mental age ten years and three months. Single. Walks, talks, tidy. American. Catholic. Moron. Reads and writes. Immoral behavior. Sex promiscuity. Has had three illegitimate children. Suggestible, easily discouraged, grudgeful and self-centered. Somewhat inclined to act on impulse and to be confused in difficult new situations. Actual residence, Providence. Committed by Eighth District Court. Transferred from State Infirmary.

January 4, 1923

Dr. Ladd,

I am answering your note to tell you the truth. Mr. Lowe didn't tell me anything but he has said different things to my mother about me when she came out to see me. She will tell you, but I know by putting a girl in a home different people have to say things about them. Dr. Ladd I have learned a good lesson now. I want to know if you will give me another chance, as I will do better, you'll see. Dr. my mother needs my support at home and William Cooper has promised to marry me. So I want to know if you will let me out. My mother wants me. My father is dead. I will be glad to talk with you some day. Dr. will you please let me know as I expect my mother any day now to see me. I am not like some of the girls you let out that do the same thing over again.

Please Dr. let me know by Sunday.

Cora Duffy

September 26, 1923

Dr. Ladd -

Just a word or two letting you know I received a letter from my daughter
Cora Duffy yesterday and she hasn't received any mail from me in five
weeks and I have wrote three letters to her. What is the reason she doesn't
receive my mail? I would like to know. Could you please tell me the reason
she doesn't receive them. Dr. Ladd I am thinking it is some going when
they keep the U.S. mail from you. There was a lady to my house a while
ago about Cora and you know her well. She has some scandalous talk
to my door about Cora and if you would like to know I can tell you. She
better not come there again. The truth is bad enough but when it comes to
lies I don't stand for them. I won't say more now hoping I will hear from
you and hope they don't keep this mail from you.

From Mrs. Mary Duffy

December 27, 1923

Dear sir -

Just a line asking you why my daughter Miss Cora Duffy hasn't wrote to
me. I have only received the one letter from her since she has been there.
I have wrote three or four and am still waiting for her to answer. Could
you kindly tell me the trouble why she hasn't answered. Isn't she allowed
to write or what? Please tell her to answer that letter and will you kindly
answer this letter letting me know.

Mrs. Mary Duffy

December 28, 1923

My dear Mrs. Duffy:-

Our girls are allowed to write every other Sunday as a general thing. This
month however the writing Sunday for the girls came on the Sunday just
before Christmas. Many of the girls asked if they might be allowed to write
on the Sunday after Christmas so they might tell their people about the
Christmas activities.

  Cora came to me on the 23rd of November and the 25th was writing
Sunday, and probably she did not feel like writing that day. You say you
have received one letter from her which was probably written on December
9th. Since this there has been no writing Sunday. Doubtless you will
receive a letter from her next week.

Very truly yours,
Joseph H. Ladd, Supt.

February 9, 1924

My dear Dr. Jones:-

I am enclosing a letter from Cora Duffy to Mrs. Burgess. I trust you will dispose of it as you see fit.

Very truly yours,
Joseph H. Ladd, Supt.

Undated

Dr. Ladd,

Well you know if I am married I am going to live with my mother and work for her every day. I am not going to have any more children, don't you think one is enough? I suppose that you think I could not do anything for my mother. If you want to find out if I never work on the outside please write to the RI Hospital or the Scotts Laundry on Globe Street and they will tell you I have worked and supported my mother ever since I was 14 years old, and I have worked up to five weeks before my child was born. I will promise you faithfully I will do better.

 Now Dr. Ladd for my mother's sake please let me out so I can get married. This young man that I am going to marry is all right. He works hard every day and he wants to marry me so he will give his son a name. Dr. Ladd you know for yourself if your girl fell you would want her to get married and to give the child a name, so you see that I want to. Please answer so I can let my mother know. I will promise you I will work hard like I have done before. Please answer by Wednesday so I will know. Just give me one more chance and you can see that I will write to you every week and tell you just what I have done during the weeks.

From Cora Duffy

Undated

Dr. Ladd,

I am again writing to you to ask you please let me go to be married. I will promise you faithfully I will do better. You know every mother forgives her daughter the first time. So will you please Dr. Ladd to forgive me and let me be married and be happy. I will promise you I will never have any more children. I think one is enough. Dr. Ladd for my mother's sake please give me one more chance and you will see I will do better all the time. I have always worked up to five weeks before my son was born, and Dr. Ladd will you please let me go down to see my cousin in G1, her name is Grace. Kindly let me know by Wednesday.

Oblige,
Cora Duffy

Undated

Dr. Ladd,

I have been speaking to Miss Hicks about marriage and she told me to
write to Dr. Ladd and ask him about it. The baby's father was willing to get
married and she said you should let me know and will you please let me
know now and Wednesday.

Oblige,
Cora Duffy

March 21, 1924

Dear Doctor:

We are sending you herewith all the belongings of Cora Duffy, and I cannot understand the vagaries of the human mind when they desire to leave an elysium like your own place to come to this place.

Kindly return enclosed receipt for goods delivered, and oblige.

Henry Jones, M.D.
Superintendent, Rhode Island State Infirmary

June 9, 1924

Kind sir -

I am dropping you a line regarding to my daughter Cora Duffy. Could you
kindly tell me the reason why she hasn't wrote to me. I have only received
one letter from her since I was out to see her on the 15th day of May.
Would you also kindly tell me the reason why she has to work so hard out
there. If she is feeble minded as they say I don't see why she has to work
out there. There is nothing feeble minded about her only she is wild like a
good many running around. She's out there now six months and I would
like to know how long she has to stay out there. She is my only support
and I need her home to support me and the two children. The State aint
keeping them, I am keeping them. I haven't any more to say till I hear from
you.

Please answer this letter.
Mrs. Mary Duffy

June 11, 1924

My dear Mrs. Duffy:-

I am unable to tell you why Cora does not write to you. She has the opportunity to write to you every second Sunday if she so desires.

  As you know Cora was committed to our institution by the court to remain here until in the opinion of the court she no longer required restraint. You probably know more of the steps which led up to this commitment than we do.

Very truly yours,
Joseph H. Ladd, Supt.

July 21, 1924

Kind sir -

Would you please be so kind as to let me know when my daughter Cora
Duffy is coming home as I need her so bad. I am a Civil War veteran's
widow but don't get money enough to keep me the way things are now
and pay rent. It costs so much to live. There are days when I don't have the
price of a loaf of bread and she ought to be home with me. I don't want to
say too much to you. Would you please be so kind enough to answer me. I
would go up to the State House but I am not able to get up that hill it is so
warm. Will close hoping you will please answer me.

From Mrs. Mary Duffy

August 12, 1924

My dear Miss McTernan:-

I do not find any record in our folder of your visits to Mrs. Duffy. She is
writing to have Cora come home, and I would like to have something to
refer to in regard to this matter.

Very truly yours,
Joseph H. Ladd, Supt.

August 10, 1924

Dr. Ladd,

Will you please let me know if my mother can come out on a Sunday and
see me. Also Dr. will you please let me have a chance, I will promise you
that I will do what is right. I have two places to go to right away to work.
You seen in the letter my mother needs my support badly now. Please Dr.
give me one more chance I will do better.

  Kindly let me know this week by Sunday.

Thanking you,
Cora Duffy

August 12, 1924

My dear Mrs. Duffy:-

You write asking me when Cora is coming home. Of course, you know that Cora was committed to our institution by the court, and it is probable that she was not committed to us without reason.

 Cora is doing very well here in the school, but of course there must be some valid reason for her having been sent here, and I do not feel like being responsible for her parole in the face of her court commitment. We will look the matter up, however, and perhaps we can arrange at some later date.

Very truly yours,
Joseph H. Ladd, Supt.

August 30, 1924

Dear Daughter,

Just a few lines to let you know I am well and hope you are the same. I got
home all right Saturday night only I was cold in the machine. I am all right
now. Bertha isn't home now as she is nursing her brother's wife and won't
be home for about a week yet. I haven't been any place as it has been so
hot. About a week ago there was a lady here to see me. She said she was
from Exeter School and she lives in Providence. She has scandalous talk
about you and I'll tell you when I see you. It is bad enough to tell the truth
but when it comes to a pack of lies I won't stand for it. I haven't much
news to tell you. Harrie has moved over to the East Side, Fox Point. Jennie
was over today.

  I'm sending you a newspaper and gum and I'll send the belt later. I
haven't any more now to tell you until I see you. Monday is Labor Day and
Charlie and Lillian are well and could be better than I am. I will now close
hoping to hear from you soon.

From,
Your mother

October 6, 1924

My dear Mrs. Duffy:-

If Cora has failed to receive any letters which have come to her it is on account of their containing something which we considered would tend to make her more discontented.

In regard to the visiting of the woman to whom you refer I think I am safe in assuring you that she will not call on you again for so long as Cora is in the school there will be no occasion for her to call on you.

Very truly yours,
Joseph H. Ladd, Supt.

November 7, 1924

My dear Father Farrelly:-

Herewith is a note to you from Cora Duffy, who was committed to our
institution. I have had our social worker look the matter up quite carefully,
and from the things we find it does not seem to be advisable to allow Cora
to go home.

Very truly yours,
Joseph H. Ladd, Supt.

January 2, 1925

My dear Doctor:

Mrs. Mary Duffy, mother of Cora Duffy, has called in again with regard to her daughter who is an inmate of your institution.

Mrs. Duffy is getting along in years and feels the need of help and is very anxious to have Cora with her.

Will you kindly give me a report on the condition of Cora and advise me the likelihood of her release?

Any information you can give me relative to the above will be greatly appreciated and I will get in touch with Mrs. Duffy immediately.

Very truly yours,
Louis W. Brown
Attorney and Counselor at Law

January 7, 1925

My dear Mr. Brown:-

According to our records there has been a long series of sexual
irregularities in the case of Cora Duffy.

   Mrs. Duffy seems to be a rather erratic, obsteperous sort of woman, who
is not well fitted to control Cora.

   Cora herself is an easy-going, good dispositioned mental defective of an
intelligence rating of 58%.

   I do not consider it advisable to allow Cora to go home.

Very truly yours,
Joseph H. Ladd, Supt.

January 25, 1925

Dr. Ladd,

Will you please give me a chance out in the world. I will promise you I will do better than before. Has the judge seen you yet? Please let me know. Dr. Ladd I will promise you I will work as what I have done before and I am willing to keep all the promises I make to you.

Please answer and let me know this week.

P.S. my mother needs my support more now than ever.

From Cora Duffy

January 28, 1925

Cora Duffy:-

You were sent to the institution because in the judgment of the court it
was necessary for you to be sent here. Your mother is making herself very
disagreeable in regard to the matter of your being in the school, and does
not seem to be a proper person to take care of you, so I think until the
court directs you to be sent home you will have to make the best of it.

Dr. Ladd

February 4, 1925

Kind sir -

I am taking the pleasure of writing to you again. I wrote to my daughter
Cora Monday the 2nd and would you be so kind as to let me know if she
received that letter. I don't say anything in my letters to her about anybody
that they should keep her mail from her. Although I would like to say a
lot of things to her but if I put in anything I care about she don't get it
or if she puts anything in her letters they won't send them to me. Could
you please tell me the reason for them keeping her mail I send her and for
them having to read all letters to her and those she sends me. I would like
to know when she is coming home. I think she has served long enough for
what she has done. What she done she done to herself and me, nobody
else.

  You know as well as I do there is nothing the matter with her head. Only
you just put her there for punishment and I am the one that is suffering
for it. I don't mean to say anything about anybody or against anybody. But
my positions are worn out. I can say as Christ said when he was on earth.
Those who has not committed sin can take up the first stone and throw
it. That was a wicked woman who was on earth. But there were no stones
throwed. They all committed sin and they couldn't throw any. Her sins
when she made her first confession was all forgiven as pure as the day she
was baptised. I don't know whether you're a Catholic or a Protestant but I
am a Catholic thank God. That's the sweetest thing to be.

  I don't think I will say any more to you for fear I might say too much.

From Mrs. Mary Duffy

Undated

Dr. Ladd,

Will you please let me know if I can't go out in a family. I have tried so
hard to be home and have a good report every month so I want to know
if you will be so kind to give me six months parole and you will see what
kind of a girl I am.

  Kindly give me a chance and please let me know.

From Cora Duffy

February 12, 1925

My dear Mrs. Duffy:-

I am afraid that you have the wrong idea as to the reason why Cora was sent over here. She was not sent here for punishment for anything that she has done, but for the reason that she does not seem to be able to keep from doing these things. It is considered that her mind is not quite right or she would not persist in doing the things she does do.

In regard to your letters to Cora, I am sorry to say that most of them are not delivered to her. In every letter you write to her you either have some very unkind things to say about somebody or tell her some harrowing tale or other to make her discontented. If Cora is to stay here I see no reason why she should not have all the chance there is to be contented.

If it gives you any pleasure to find fault with me or anybody else in connection with Cora's being here, I am perfectly willing you should write to me any kind of letters you wish, but I must insist that the letters you write to Cora be free from fault finding and complaining.

The probability is when Cora has reached an age at which she will be incapable of bearing children she will be paroled, but probably not before that time.

Very truly yours,
Joseph H. Ladd, Supt.

February 17, 1925

Dear Dr. Ladd,

As had been hinted to me previous to my interview with you and as I
anticipated would happen when the relatives learned that you did not favor
a parole for Cora Duffy, their attorney has petitioned the Eighth District
Court for her dismissal.

Although they know my feeling in the case they have asked me to testify
giving Cora the benefit of the doubt wherever it might arise. This I have
agreed to do and so on Thursday a task lies before me in the role of a
diplomatic witness.

I am thus informing you in regard to my position lest you may think my
opinion has been changed since our talk.

I also take this opportunity Doctor, of thanking you for your most kind
and courteous interview and I do hope I shall again have the pleasure of
talking with you.

With my warm regards, I remain,

Sincerely yours,
E.A. McLaughlin, M.D.

February 24, 1925

My dear Doctor McLaughlin:-

I received your letter of February 17th concerning the case of Cora Duffy. It is simply the matter of difference of opinion. The courts are entrusted to decide which opinion is to prevail. I shall expect to see you on Thursday.

Very truly yours,
Joseph H. Ladd, Supt.

February 24, 1925

My dear Mr. Lowe:-

Application has been made to the 8th District Court for the discharge
of Cora Duffy to her mother. The hearing on this is set for two o'clock
Thursday afternoon, February 26th, at the court house in Knightsville.

On this account I shall be unable to be at the State House on Thursday.

Very truly yours,
Joseph H. Ladd, Supt.

April 21, 1925

My dear Miss McTernan:-

The Duffy case is in the air again. Will you please send to Mr. Putnam a résumé of your findings in the case?

Very truly yours,
Joseph H. Ladd, Supt.

April 19, 1925

Mrs. Ladd,

Will you please get me 25 cents worth of mixed hard candy. Also Mrs.
Ladd when Dr. Merry comes this week please may I see her as you know
what I told you when I went to court my side is getting worse than better.

  Kindly let me know by Tuesday.

From Cora Duffy

April 21, 1925

My dear Mr. Putnam:-

In response to your request I am sending the following in regard to Cora
Duffy.

Cora Duffy was born November 11, 1895. She has an intelligence
quotient of 58, and in her work just about lives up to this intelligence
quotient. Her school history bears out the same thing. She has had three
illegitimate children, two of whom are living with Cora's mother and the
other at the State Home and School, I think. It was reported that she
showed undue interest in the opposite sex when she was going to school.
She seems to me to be a quiet, well-behaved, good natured, feeble-minded
woman, who required constant supervision on account of her good nature.
The psychologist reports her as being distinctly an institutional case.

Cora was committed to us on November 23, 1923 by the Eighth District
Court. On February 25, 1925 she was again bought before the Court with
the idea of having her discharged.

The Court remanded her to the institution.

Very truly yours,
Joseph H. Ladd, Supt.

April 22, 1925

My dear Mr. Putnam:

Dr. Ladd has asked me to send you a summary on the above mentioned
patient. All that I can say could be summed up in one sentence - The girl is
where she belongs.

As I have not the notes at home I can only give you approximate dates.
She was committed to us from the State Infirmary where she had given
birth to her third illegitimate child. This was in the fall of 1923, I think.

I called on the mother, a woman of perhaps 60, living under the most
squalid conditions on Thurber Avenue, herself, her kitchen, clothing and
bedclothes DIRTY. It was with some difficulty that she let me in. I have
since been told that most people only get to her front door steps. She was
extremely saucy, reviling Miss Cook for having Cora sent to us, declaring
that if it were not for her deceased husband - a Civil War veteran - that we
would not have our soft chairs in the State House. I forgot, she was also
very abusive in regard to Mr. Lowe.

She would not let me in to a bedroom to see Cora's girl, aged 5 at the
time. The child was sick and I reported to the District Nurses. She told me
that Cora's boy, William aged 8 then and who was lying on a filthy couch
in the kitchen, attended Thurber Avenue School.

On calling the school I learned he was known as William Peartree (the
name of the putative father), that his parents were dead and that he was
being brought up by his grandmother. I told the teacher who his mother
was and she remembered the girl well.

Cora had not done well in school. When she was 12 years old she was
ready to enter the 4th grade and was sent to another school. The Thurber
Ave. teachers heard nothing further.

While calling on Mrs. Duffy I tried gently to put over the reason why Cora had been sent to us - Society must protect itself against nameless children and our School gave the protection. I also told her not to expect to ever have Cora come home.

I called at the church rectory and talked with the priest assigned to Thurbers Ave. He had never been allowed into the house and as far as he knew only Mrs. Duffy and her daughter (not Cora) lived there. Nothing was known of William in the Sunday School.

Some months later Miss Keefe, Mothers' Aid Dept., told me that Mrs. Duffy had applied for Mother's Aid, claiming she was acting "in loco parentis." When Miss Keefe called, Mrs. Duffy gave her the usual harangue about "people who are paid to mind other peoples' business." This time I was included in the tale. However, Mrs. Duffy said, "You might know she was Irish, she was so smooth tongued about it." Miss Keefe went to the church. The Pastor advised that no aid be given and that the woman should give up the children.

Almost a year ago Mrs. Duffy went to the School saying she was coming down at a later date and take Cora home. Dr. Ladd was not at the School that day. I went to the home (and got to front steps, only) and told the woman in no uncertain language that she would not get the girl home, telling her that I guessed I was too gentle at my former visit. She closed the door on me saying, "You think you are so smart, well I am going to take her home next visiting day myself."

Mr. Ernest Hardy, whose son is a patient here and who was janitor at the Oxford Street School when I taught there, asked me one day more than a year ago if we ever got a Cora Shannon from Thurber Ave. I told him it was Cora Duffy and that we had her. He told me she had attended the evening school some years before and he had his hands full keeping her from "throwing herself on the boys" as he expressed it. I told the mother this story on my second visit, refusing to give her the man's name or his occupation. I told her he had a son, a patient. Naturally, she was much incensed. To be frank I was not sorry, because she understood me perfectly then.

I have since been told that William Peartree has been sent to the special school for defectives on Public Street. He must be pretty defective because there are only a few of these places of last resort, the majority of backward children being looked after in their own school building in a special room. As for the little girl I know nothing. I have talked with the SPCC and they say they can do nothing, as the grandmother feeds and clothes the children and often calls at the schools in regard to them.

Please do not consider letting the girl out. Ask Miss Cook. She knows.

Respectfully,
Miss Mary F. McTernan,
Social Worker, Exeter School

July 13, 1925

Dr. Ladd,

Will you please tell me the reason you don't let me have my mail when
you receive it and my mother tells me she hasn't heard from me in three
months. It is pretty funny, I write every other Sunday. Instead of making
me happy it is making me worse, there is enough of lies told on me now
and you know it. I am so discouraged I can't do anything but the right
things. I haven't ran away from here yet, but Dr. Ladd if I don't at least
have a trial or get my mother's mail I will do something. Please let me
know this week.

From Cora Duffy

P.S. Dr. Ladd I mean everything I say.

August 23, 1925

Dr. Ladd,

I am again writing to you to ask you if you will please give me one more
chance you see I have been good and have good reports so at least Dr. Ladd
you could put me out on trial. When I went to court they all were willing
to give me one more chance but you, and I am not so feebleminded as
you think I am. If I can work and slave in the school I can do the same on
the outside. And another thing is Dr. Ladd I don't belong here as I am a
House of Corrections case. After my child was born they wanted me at the
Seven Station in Providence. I didn't do anything out of the way only over
one quart of milk. When I see you I can tell you don't want to give me at
least one trial. Can I go home on two weeks vacation so I can settle my
trouble. Please Dr. give me one more chance. I don't want to run away and
spoil my record but if you don't let me go I will have to do something as I
have done my punishment a year ago. Please let me know. Dr. Ladd I am
so discouraged I could run away this minute I am writing to you.

Please answer.

Yours truly,
Cora Duffy

August 30, 1925

Miss Murphy,

Will you please forgive me for what I said last Monday night as I am quiet
and didn't mean to be so sassy to you. I will do anything you want me
to do. Miss Murphy I have been good ever since I came here. Only last
Monday night when A. Germain had put things in my head about running
away.

Yours truly,
Cora Duffy

October 4, 1925

Dr. Ladd,

Will you please let me have my eyes seen to my glasses. One not strong and
I have a lot of headaches. Will you please let me know if I can go to my
brother's to live. He wants me, also my sister-in-law. I can behave myself. I
have good reports just the same every month. You told me to keep up my
good reports and in a short while you said I could go out. I think two long,
long worried years are long enough to stay here. I know the difference from
wrong now. So please trust me for one chance. Kindly let me know this
week.

From Cora Duffy

Please answer.

February 1, 1926

Dear Doctor:-

You will remember the case of Cora Duffy whom her parents were so anxious to separate from the custody of the school. Her counsel, Mr. George J. Eastman has been pressing us for another hearing stating that he has now made arrangements whereby continuous supervision of Cora can be maintained in her home.

We have tentatively agreed upon Thursday, February 4 at 2:00 P.M. at the Cranston District Court as a day for hearing this matter once more.

I endeavored to reach you by telephone today but the line was not in good working order, and I am therefore writing to inquire if you can be present at Court on Thursday P.M.

I would appreciate you notifying this office as to whether you can be present or not.

Yours very truly,
Harold E. Staples
Fourth Assistant Attorney General

February 4, 1926

Dear Dr. Ladd,

After talking over the Cora Duffy affair with you yesterday I bethought me
that Judge Brown and his wife were very friendly with one of my married
sisters and her husband. So today at 8 A.M. I phone him telling him I was
Mrs. McElroy's sister. I gave him the entire social history as I know it, plus
a lot of personal things that are only hinted at in my writeup, also I told
him what Monsignor Farrelly told Miss Keefe of Mother's Aid in regard
to Mrs. Duffy and her incompetency to take care of the two children. I
told him Miss Keefe and I had taken it up with the SPCC but were told
nothing could be done because to all appearances the children were
being adequately cared for. I told him what Mrs. Duffy had written you
in regard to Cora's sins being forgiven and the erroneous impression she
tried to convey. Judge Brown agreed that such testimony would be rather
difficult to bring out in court and was very grateful for it. He asked me to
come to his office and talk over the matter with him as "the lawyer for the
defendant may have as many hearings as he wishes to ask for and I want
to know this case still better." He told me he was on the point of phoning
the lawyers, when I called, that he did not want to case brought up today
because he thought it unfair to take you such a distance. If there is any way
that I can prevent that girl's going out I am willing to do it. I am enclosing
the notes I used when talking with the Judge. No need to keep them but
you can see how I covered all phases of it. In case Judge Brown does decide
to release Cora I think you should have Mr. Staples tell the Judge that
Cora's baby will be turned over to her to care for. I see no reason why the
State should keep that baby. It is or was at the State Home and School.

Miss Mary F. McTernan

February 4, 1926

Dear Dr. Ladd:

I am anxious to explain my attitude regarding Cora Duffy. I do not want you to feel that I am going over your head and force you to do anything that fails to comport with you idea of duty and justice.

It is my honest belief that Cora Duffy under the constant supervision of her relatives will be as well off and more useful to the community than she would be confined to the Exeter School. Whatever interest the state may have to correct improper tendencies can hardly balance the right that citizens enjoy under natural law.

I am merely writing this letter to you as a matter of courtesy. Do not think that I am criticizing or complaining regarding your treatment. It is my understanding of the matter that Cora Duffy has received the same treatment from your hand as that afforded to all persons placed under your immediate charge. I merely desire to state that it is my opinion that she will be better off under the conditions which I intend to explain to the court, and at the same time relieve the state from an unnecessary burden.

I know that you will not use this letter against our interest because I send it to you in the spirit of professional courtesy.

Respectfully yours,
George J. Eastman
Counselor and Attorney at Law

February 6, 1926

My dear Mr. Eastman:-

Your letter of February 4th concerning the Duffy case is received. I beg
to assure you that I have absolutely no personal feelings in this matter
whatever. I believe that it is not a good thing to have too many girls of the
type of Cora Duffy in the community.

I know that she is a mentally defective girl. I know she wasn't properly
taken care of in the past, and I doubt if she will be in the future. I simply
state these things to the Judge. The law provides that the Judge has
authority to discharge a case from this institution if he sees fit to do so. If
he discharges the case it relieves me of all responsibility. I have nothing to
gain by keeping he girl in the institution, and the institution has nothing
to gain by keeping her here. The State has provided through its legislature
that the Judge may discharge cases, therefore I see no reason why I should
be disturbed over this matter in any way.

Very truly yours,
Joseph H. Ladd, Supt.

March 5, 1926

Dear Sir:-

Mr. Eastman is now asking to have this case heard before Judge Brown at the Cranston Probate Court on Thursday, March 11 at 2:00 P.M., which is agreeable to me, if so to you.

If for any reason this is not convenient, will you let me know and I will arrange to have the matter put over.

Very truly yours,
Harold E. Staples
Fourth Assistant Attorney General

Undated

Dr. Ladd,

How long will it be before you will let me out again? The two times I went
to the court I never heard the Judge say anything about me staying here
at the School. The doctors that put me here are all willing to give me one
more chance but you weren't. Dr. Ladd the only thing I ever done was
having children and there are other girls you let out that has done worse
than I ever thought of doing. I have good reports every month and you see
how hard I work down at the service building. I am here three years and
it is long enough to be shut up and have received a good long lesson. You
could put me out on six months trial. I never have hit any of the employees
and never have run away and I see you are letting a lot of the girls out that
has run away. If I start and cut up perhaps you will let me out. I see the
girls that behave stay here and the girls cut up you let out. If you don't
let me out soon you will be very sorry and I mean every word I say. If you
think I am going to stay here 12 or 13 years you are mistaken. If I can work
for the State, I can work for my mother and my children.

Oblige,
Cora Duffy

September 5, 1926

Mrs. Ladd,

I am writing to you and tell you I am going to turn a new leaf over and will
try and be better and see what will turn up for me. I am so discouraged
and I would feel much easier when I have my side tended to. I think that if
I have it fixed I wouldn't act this way at times and if my dear mother would
write to me often I would be much better also, and my dear son that is over
at the State Home and School. I have a lot on my mind to think about. I
am so discouraged.

From Cora Duffy

Will you please answer and let me know what I will do.

October 21, 1926

My dear Mrs. Duffy:-

Cora is complaining a good deal about a pain in her side and seems to
think she requires an operation. I would like to have your permission to
take her to the hospital and have the operation performed if it is found
necessary.

Very truly yours,
Joseph H. Ladd, Supt.

October 21, 1926

Gentlemen:-

Cora Duffy is complaining a good deal about a pain in her side and seems
to think she requires an operation. I would like to have your permission
to take her to the hospital and have the operation performed if it is found
necessary.

Very truly yours,
Joseph H. Ladd, Supt.

October 25, 1926

Dear Dr. Ladd:

In answer to your letter of the 21st in regard to Cora Duffy, an inmate of
your institution, I would suggest that you call in Dr. Merry or any other
competent physician or surgeon whom you desire as a consultant and
have an examination made of this patient. If in your opinion and that of
the physician called in it is necessary to perform an operation, this is your
authority for so doing.

Sincerely,
Louis H. Putnam
Director of State Institutions

October 25, 1926

Dear sir,

I received your letter this morning and I am very sorry to hear my daughter doesn't feel good. If it is necessary for the operation I'd just as soon let her have it because she has been complaining of her side for some time. Please let me know the day and the hospital she will have it done at as I would like to know. I want to be with her when she goes under the knife. Please be sure and let me know.

Thanking you for notifying me.

I am sincerely,
Mrs. Duffy

December 30, 1926

My dear Dr. Briggs:-

Can you tell me anything about the mental level of Charles Francis Duffy, who I understand is in your institution? His mother, Cora, is an inmate here. There are two other children that I understand are defective and I am wondering about Charles.

Very truly yours,
Joseph H. Ladd, Supt.

January 3, 1927

My dear Dr. Ladd:

Concerning Charles Francis Duffy and your inquiry received this morning, this child is placed out and the records are, of course, in the Children's Bureau. I am referring your letter to them.

Please accept our very best wishes for yourself and family for the coming year.

Very truly yours,
A.S. Briggs
Superintendent, State Home and School

January 6, 1927

My dear Dr. Ladd:

Your letter to Dr. Briggs, Superintendent of the State Home and School, was referred to me for a reply.

William Duffy has been in a family home for two years. So far he shows little sign of defective mentality. He is an active busy child with a strong will and temper, ver inquisitive and has a tendency to roam. We will try to have the boy examined later on and send you a report.

Hoping this brief report is of service to you, I am

Very truly yours,
Anna Griffith
Director, Children's Bureau

February 21, 1927

To His Honor Judge Louis W. Brown:

At your suggestion I have, on February 17, 1927 examined Cora Duffy, an inmate at the State School for Feebleminded in Exeter, Rhode Island.

As this case has occasioned considerable home, institutional, and Medico-Legal interest, it might be well to take up this case in some length in order that the reasons for her detention at the Exeter School be shown forth.

Her mental condition as shown by her school record of dullness, and reports of sex proclivities, presaged social difficulties later on.

These were made manifest by her having an illegitimate child while yet in her teens. Later on this was repeated, and with the same man. This fact might be, and probably is, being placed to her credit, by some, showing her "fidelity and natural weakness for her first lover as is sometimes shown by other women of normal mentality." Four years later this situation of illegitimacy arose with a different man.

In the meantime, she had been under some form of suggestive supervision. This was not sufficient to safeguard her, and keep her away from designing persons. She is therefore at an early age, found to be the mother of three illegitimate children without being able to support one.

They therefore were a burden to others, either the municipality, the State, or the relatives.

In the person of relative, the mother of Cora assumed to try the role of caretaker of the children and the supervision of Cora.

This was entirely unsatisfactory for these reasons:

First - The mental attitude of the mother toward the problem, as evinced by her reasoning, i.e., punishment for sin.

Second - The feeblemindedness of Cora.

Third - The economic incompetency of both parties.

During her last pregnancy, Cora came under the care and control of the
State, at the State Infirmary, at Howard, RI, where she remained until
upon the presentation of certificates of being Feebleminded signed by
John E. O'Donnel, M.D. and myself. She was presented before you, and by
you, committed to the Exeter School where she has since remained.

Her release from that institution has been repeatedly sought for,
principally on these grounds:

First - Her economic worth at home to help support her children and
aging mother.

Second - "That she has been sufficiently punished."

In my opinion either or both of these demands are not sufficient to
warrant her discharge for these reasons. In regard to the economic value of
Cora as a supportive agent in her home, I have well known, and you have
been informed by the Superintendant of the School, Dr. Ladd, that her
earning power is small, that she would have to be under supervision and
direction, and that she lacks initiative to compete with others.

On the grounds of "being punished enough," we can see clearly the utter
fallacy of trying to reason with one obsessed with this institutional, or
punitive psychosis.

Through her early training, or suggestions of both combined, Cora views
her detention as a matter of punishment for sin, and that her four years
detention is sufficient to repay to society her social obligations.

Her views on that subject alone were unchangeable as you made
clear in your conversation with her, and must convince you that she is
feebleminded.

Somewhere a suggestion has been made to Cora that she could "be let out from the School" if she submitted to an operation. This operation she asks for in a letter to the Superintendent of the School. This petition she claims not to have known of. She evidently does not know what this operation is, what it does, or what it implies.

Her answers to you on this question, I am sure must further convince you that (for a woman going through the periods of three conceptions and birth of children her lack of knowledge of what she asks for in the way of operation) she is feebleminded.

In my examination of February 17, 1927, I found Cora less emotional than at other periods, also that her physical condition is good.

I am still of the opinion however, that she is feebleminded, and that supervision of the state should be exercised over her until:

First - She is not able to bear children because of age.

Second - She is given the benefit of sterilization by operation or by X-ray.

As the inmate has in all probability a period of 10-12 more years of ovarian fertility, you can readily determine the responsibility that the State assumes in discharging this inmate (and others in a similar mental condition.)

With the disproportionate increase of mental defectives over the normal population such a case as Cora Duffy should not even be paroled until a satisfactory environment is found. Such environment should mean kindliness, occupational improvement, and a vigorous control and constant intelligent supervision. If such is for Cora Duffy, I would respectfully recommend, that your Honor parole, but not discharge, her, even though she has been committed as feebleminded.

Respectfully submitted,
Henry A. Jones, M.D.

March 5, 1927

My dear Dr. Jones:-

Much obliged for the copy of the report on Cora Duffy which you sent me.
It seems to me you have gone into this thing very fully and carefully.

Very truly yours,
Joseph H. Ladd, Supt.

June 22, 1927

Dr. Ladd,

I first called on a friend who lives on Hope Street not far from Goulding St. The latter is a small lane running from Wickenden to Transit. It is between East and Governor.

This friend did not know the people, but said there is a tough crowd on that street. The police were called out in the middle of the night awhile ago.

I then rode around the district. There are three or four dreadfully shabby houses in the lane. I did not call but instead went to Capt. Pelrine at the 3rd Precinct. He authorized the night man, who has covered that beat for a long time and whom he had awakened, to give me the following story:

"Duffy is a heavy drinker, so is his wife. Her sisters live upstairs. We have been watching the house for a long time because we knew they have parties there. A few nights ago around one or two A.M. we cleaned the place out getting three men. I certainly think it is no place for anybody to live."

In view of this statement and the permission of the police to use it, it seemed futile to make any visit. However, if the Commission wish it I can do it tomorrow, if you will phone me even though I make it at night.

Mary F. McTernan
Social Worker, Exeter School

June 23, 1927

My dear Judge Brown:

In accordance with my agreement with you I had my social worker look up
the conditions at Goulding Street. She did not visit the house, but did visit
the Third Precinct police station and Captain Pelrine authorized her to
give me a report.

  In view of this report I certainly shall not recommend Cora's parole to
this place. I am making a report of this matter to the Commission.

Very truly yours,
Joseph H. Ladd, Supt.

June 23, 1927

My dear Mr. Putnam:

On February 26, 1925 Mr. George J. Eastman brought action for the discharge of Cora Duffy. This request was refused.

On March 11, 1926 Mr. Eastman again brought the matter up and Judge Brown took the case under advisement.

Now Mr. Eastman is pressing for a decision.

The plan now is to have her paroled to her brother, who lives at Goulding Street, Providence. I asked Miss McTernan to look up the matter and she made a report authorized by Captain Pelrine of the Third Precinct.

In view of this report I certainly should not recommend that she be paroled to this place.

Mr. Eastman intends to bring action of habeas corpus before the Superior Court if Cora is not paroled. I am making this report so if the Commission wishes to avoid this action it may do so, but my opinion is that it would be better to let the thing go through if Mr. Eastman insists on it.

Very truly yours,
Joseph H. Ladd, Supt.

June 25, 1927

My dear Mr. Eastman:

It is our understanding that you are interested in the case of Cora Duffy,
an inmate of the Exeter School for Girls, and are anxious that this girl be
paroled from the institution to the care of her brother.

  The report from the Exeter School authorized by the captain of the Third
Precinct Police Station will, we feel, dissuade you from attempting to be a
party to the parole of this woman.

Very truly yours,
Louis Putnam
Director of State Institutions

August 27, 1927

My dear Dr. Sartwell:

Is there a record there of former employees? If so, would it be too much trouble for you to look up Cora Duffy and see what the record is?

  She tells me she used to work at the hospital, and wants to return.

Yours truly,
Joseph H. Ladd, Supt.

August 31, 1927

Dear Doctor:

I have your letter relative to Cora Duffy and will say in reply that if she will
let us know under whom she worked and in what year, we will endeavor
to find her record. We have looked through our files and cannot find the
name of Miss Duffy listed as that of a former attendant.

Very truly yours,
Ransom H. Sartwell
Superintendant, State Hospital for Mental Diseases

September 18, 1927

Miss McTurney,

I am so sorry what I said to Sadie Robinson as she has put lies to it all.
I told her that you explain about being out six months and I said you
happen to say her name and Flora B. You don't know how bad I feel about
it, so will you please forgive me as it will never happen again. I will promise
you.

From,
Cora Duffy

September 20, 1927

My dear Dr. Sartwell:

I find that the Cora Duffy I wrote you about recently worked at the State
Hospital under the name of Cora Peartree. She claims she worked there in
the spring of 1919.

Very truly yours,
Joseph H. Ladd, Supt.

September 22, 1927

Dear Doctor:

I have the record of Cora, and she it seems worked here for a short time in 1918. "Left without notice, fair worker" is what is recorded on her card.

Very truly yours,
Ransom H. Sartwell
Superintendant, State Hospital for Mental Diseases

February 24, 1928

Dear Cora,

Just a few lines to let you know I am well hoping you are the same. I
received your letter and was glad to hear from you. I guess I will tell you
that Lillian was down to the Rhode Island Hospital for six weeks. She is
down to Crawford Island. Do not worry about her, she is all right. She had
appendicitis and had not dared to tell you because you would be upset. She
went in January and got out February 22.

 I will send you the stockings as soon as I get paid.

From,
Mother

July 5, 1928

Doctor,

Mrs. Simmons, at RI Hospital, will write you a lengthy letter on Cora. Cora will not be reemployed because of 3 illegitimate children.

Mrs. Simmons suggested seeing other hospitals.

Miss McT.

July 6, 1928

Dear Cora,

Just a few lines to let you know I am well hoping you are the same. I am
sending these things to you now because in the middle of the month I
did not have enough change. I hope you will get this box. I do not know
when I will be out because I do not know when they will take me out. Mrs.
Andrews is going to take a vacation for one week. If you were home I could
take you too. You are out there five years. They are making you work like
a slave and for the State. I would not care if you could come home for one
month during the year. You are out there long enough to take a vacation.
You are out there because you did not mind, I call to the office the next
to last time I was over there with a message and he was not around, so
I gave it to Miss Reed and he did not give me my answer and that is an
unpleasant thing to do. Next Sunday is your writing Sunday and I hope
you will write.

From,
Mother

August 20, 1928

My dear Mrs. Duffy,

Cora has been asking for a long time for a vacation, and I don't see any particular reason why she shouldn't have one.

If you want her to come home for two weeks and will agree to bring her back at the end of two weeks without any trouble you may come and get her.

I don't see any reason why she shouldn't get along for two weeks all right.

Very truly yours,
Joseph H. Ladd, Supt.

August 23, 1928

Kind sir,

I received your letter and was glad to hear from you and was also glad to
hear that Cora is coming home on her vacation. My son in law is very
nervous and the Dr. said he could not drive the machine. I will try and
come out Saturday or Sunday. If I do not come then it will be next week
after.

Yours truly,
Mrs. Duffy

August 24, 1928

To the Honorable Louis W. Brown:

Dear Sir,

Since you have so much to do with the Duffy case I thought you might be
interested to know I have given Mrs. Duffy permission to take Cora home
for two weeks' vacation, so if you happen to see her on the streets you will
know why.

Very truly yours,
Joseph H. Ladd, Supt.

August 28, 1928

Dear Dr. Ladd,

I am writing you a few lines to let you know I got home all right and was
so pleased to be at home and I think I have learned one good long lesson.
I do not go out anywhere and I don't intend to and my mother thanks you
very much for giving me the two weeks and I will return when my time is
up. Tell Mrs. Bennett that I will write to her later.

 I am thanking you very much for giving me two weeks. I was telling
mother I hoped I will be home next summer for good as she needs my help
now more than ever, as she is getting older now and needs my money.

Kindly oblige,
Cora Duffy

February 5, 1929

Dear Cora:

I am sorry that I did not see you before I left. I am feeling all right. How
are all the girls? I thought I was going to the Lying In Hospital but I am at
the State Infirmary instead. How is the attendant in ward fifteen? I would
like to see her.

   Don't forget to write. I miss you very much.

   This is all I can think of now so I will close.

Love,
Ora

February 14, 1929

Dear friend,

Just a line to let you know I am well hope you are the same. I am still walking around. How is Marion and Ella? I am awful lonesome here without you. How is Virginia? Tell the French girl with the black hair the attendant I was asking for her. Did you have a good time on the 12th of February? Lucy and I are here together and are having a fine time. Did you get the first letter I wrote to you? Don't forget to answer me and put a word in for Lucy. Good-by and good luck to all the girls there.

Ora

February 24, 1929

Kind sir:

I thought I would drop you a note as I was writing to Cora. Cora was
speaking about a vacation this summer as she told me in the last letter. I
hope Cora will be home all summer as I need her for good. She is always
speaking about her side. I think it would be a good thing to send her to the
hospital. What do you think about it? I guess that is all for present.

Mrs. Duffy

March 7, 1929

My dear Mrs. Duffy:

I am sorry that Cora seems to have so much trouble with her side, but
I doubt if it is a thing that anything can be done for. We have a woman
physician visiting her every other week, and she has seen Cora from time
to time and reported to me that she was unable to find anything. Without
doubt Cora may have a little pain in her side from a previous operation,
but I doubt if anything in the surgical way could be done about it.

  I see no reason why Cora shouldn't have a vacation next summer. She
had one last summer, and so far as I know behaved very well, but I am not
so sure about the advisability of letting her stay all summer or letter her be
paroled for good.

Very truly yours,
Joseph H. Ladd, Supt.

March 10, 1929

Kind sir:

I received your letter and was glad to hear from you. As Cora has been away from her mother six years this May and I think that she has learned her lesson. So as I am alone so long I have nothing else but my money from the State and that is little. So I think that she ought to be out on parole for good. All I need her for is in the house for to do my work. I guess I will not say anymore but good night and God bless you.

From,
Mrs. Duffy

Undated

Dr. Ladd,

When my mother came out here a few weeks ago I asked her those things
in which you told me and she said if you place me out in a family she will
not bother me. As long as I came out in the world working she will not
bother me any more. There is lots of work if you will only let me go. Please
may I go this summer for a month instead of two weeks?

Oblige,
Cora Duffy

April 12, 1929

Kind sir:

I thought I would drop you a line and tell you that I got a letter from Cora. I told her I would write to Dr. Ladd and tell him that if you could come home for the summer or for good as I need her help. I am going out soon and if you would be so kind to drop me a letter and tell me when would the best time for her to come home I will be sure to take good care of her.

Very truly yours,
Mrs. Duffy

April 19, 1929

My dear Mrs. Duffy:

Cora got along so well on her vacation last summer I see no reason why she shouldn't go out for two weeks this summer. I cannot promise anything more than that, however.

Very truly yours,
Joseph H. Ladd, Supt.

July 7, 1929

I hereby promise to return Cora Duffy to Exeter School on August 4, 1929.

Signed,
Mary Duffy

July 14, 1929

Dr Ladd,

I am writing you these few lines as my mother has asked me to. Dr. Ladd
there is a big day August 5, Grand Army Day, and they are all going down
river and the widows are also going. So my mother has asked me if you will
let me stay a week longer so I can go with her and others. I am supposed
to come back August 4 and the 5th is that big day. I am behaving myself. I
stay in the house, I do not go out unless someone else goes with me.

   When I come back to the school I would like to have a talk with you as I
have found the truth in things.

   I was offered a good job but my mother said I could not have it as I will
not be home long enough to have it. I hope that you please let me have a
week longer. Please answer Dr. Ladd so I will know.

Thanking you,
Cora Duffy

July 20, 1929

My dear Cora:

I received your letter of July 14th concerning remaining home another week.

I thought we had agreed that this year you were not going to ask for any extension of time.

However, if this August 5th is to be such a wonderful day, I am willing that you remain home for that day, and come back on August 6th.

Very truly yours,
Joseph H. Ladd, Supt.

September 1, 1929

Dear Cora,

Just a few lines to let you know I am well hoping you are the same. Mrs.
Adams is in Newport for one week and she is well. Jennie and Lewis
and the baby was over last night. I have not much news to tell you. I am
sending you the writing paper so next Sunday is your writing Sunday.
School is open now and the children are out of my way. I have had a letter
from home and everyone is well. I guess I will come to a close. I wrote a
letter to my friend and I have got no answer.

From Mother

April 22, 1930

Kind sir:

I thought I would write to you and ask if Cora is coming home. I really
need her at home, she is 7 years away from me.

Please write to me and let me know.

From,
Mrs. Duffy

May 8, 1930

My dear Mrs. Duffy:

I suspect that we shall allow Cora to come home on a vacation some time
in July, and if she can get a job and behave herself we probably shall let her
stay there.

   This action on our part, however, if we take it, is more or less on the
line of an experiment, and Cora's success will depend to quite an extent
on your attitude. If you express to Cora the opinions you used to express
to her, namely, that everybody is wrong and she is right, Cora will not
get along. On the other hand if you back us up and tell Cora that we are
right and she is wrong and she has got to do as we tell her she may make a
success of her parole.

Very truly yours,
Joseph H. Ladd, Supt.

June 25, 1930

My dear Mrs. Duffy:

Will you definitely secure a job for Cora, let us know what it is, where it is,
how much pay she will get, etc. When you have done this we will take up
the matter of her parole.

Very truly yours,
Joseph H. Ladd, Supt.

July 5, 1930

My dear Mrs. Duffy:

You may come and get Cora a week from Sunday, July 13th.

Very truly yours,
Joseph H. Ladd, Supt.

July 14, 1930

Dear Dr. Ladd,

I am writing to you tonight to inform you that this morning I went out
looking for a job so now Dr. I found one. The name of the place is the
New Way Laundry on Baker and Allens Ave and it is piece work. The boss
said in a few that I will be all right. Now Dr. if you will let me remain out I
will do what is right. So Dr. Ladd please send me my sweater, pictures and
the home dresses that are left at the school. What State clothes I have I will
send back by mail.

Thanking you,

Kindly oblige,
Cora Duffy

July 23, 1930

My dear Miss McTernan:

Will you please go over and look up Cora Duffy. She tells me she has secured a satisfactory job, and wants to remain on parole.

I certainly shall be glad to have her remain on parole, if it is true that she has a good job in the proper locality.

Very truly yours,
Joseph H. Ladd, Supt.

July 25, 1930

Dr. Ladd,

Cora did not have a job. She has offers of two - one at the RIH laundry, the mother says, though I doubt it after what the woman in charge told me two years ago. Of course, there may be a change in supervisors. The other was at Drummonds laundry.

The mother was most cordial and never spoke about the "soft seats in the State House" won by "the Civil War veterans' fighting."

The family is moving from the hovel they have occupied 10 years. Cora is to let me know when they are settled and when she gets a job.

Miss McT

July 31, 1930

My dear friend Miss McTernan,

I thought I would drop you a few lines. We have moved yesterday morning and I went to that laundry on Sommerset Street and the boss told me to come Monday morning at 8 o'clock. So Miss McTernan if you wish you would call on 38 James St. and see my new home now. My sister and her husband helped to get things straightened up.

There is something I would like to ask you, if you will find out where my son William is as I would like to see him. Try and come to see me this week and see how you like it. If you go out to the school tell Miss Esten that I was asking for her and the girls. Well I will have to get busy and do some more work so I will say bye bye.

From yours truly,
Cora Duffy

August 27, 1930

My dear Dr. Ladd,

I thought I would drop you a line or two. I meant to write to you sooner but I have looked everywhere for work. I had a few jobs but I didn't care for them so I looked in the paper and seen an ad for a job in a hospital so I am going the first of September. They told me I had to get two references for them so the RI Hospital gave me one as I had worked there a long while ago. So Dr. Ladd I wrote to the State Hospital and they never sent me any yet. I told them all about it. So Dr. Ladd mother told me to write to you and see if you would put a good word for me as you know how I have worked for you at the school. I could do anything I put my hands to. If you would please send me a reference from the school that would be all right. I am expecting to go Monday, September 1, and the pay will be 45 dollars a month. So Dr. please help me so I can go to this place. I have been a very good girl since I came home. I seen Miss McTernan a few times. Tell Mrs. Bennett I was asking for her, also Miss Harris and Mrs. Sullivan and Ester. Please answer just as soon as you can, before Monday.

Kindly oblige,
Cora Duffy

September 20, 1930

My dear Cora:

I was very glad to receive your note of the latter part of last month. I am wondering if by any chance you have secured a permanent position yet. I hope you have been able to as certainly you need the money. Please let me hear from you some time soon.

Very truly yours,
Joseph H. Ladd, Supt.

Dear Dr. Ladd,

I received your letter and I am very pleased to hear from you. I am working
now one week ago. I am doing house work. I don't get very much pay but
when things pick up I will get more. I am getting four dollars a week, room
and board. I am left alone from six o'clock in the morning till three o'clock
in the afternoon so I have all day to do my work. Give my regards to Mrs.
Bennett, also Miss Reed and Mrs. Zonny. Dr. Ladd on my day off can I
come out some time and visit Miss Ester and the other attendants? I am
now a very good girl. I think now I am realizing the seven long years spent
at the school has done me good. Now I am knowing the right from the
wrong. I will now keep on being good.

   Tell Miss McTernan to call and see me. I am always in. Dr. Ladd have you
forgave me the way I cut up on the fourth of July as you know that I am
very quick tempered. I wouldn't have came but Rose had some white skirts
and I was trying so hard to keep them good. Write to me and tell me if I
can go out to the school and visit the attendants and see some of the girls.
I want Marion to make up with me. When I came home she got sore.

I will close my letter and will be waiting for an answer soon.

I remain as ever,
Cora Duffy

October 9, 1930

My dear Mrs. Duffy:

I am very glad to receive your nice letter and to know at last you have
secured something to do. I am told, however, that the locality in which
you are working is not a very good one. If that is the case you must be
all the more careful to watch your step to see that you don't get into any
difficulties.

 I certainly hope you can keep on working as I am sure you must need the
money. Let me hear from you whenever you feel like writing.

Very truly yours,
Joseph H. Ladd, Supt.

Undated

Miss McTernan,

I thought I would drop you a few lines. I am now doing house work. Last
Wednesday I got the job. Not much money in it but I got my room and
board. How is Dr. Ladd and the attendants at the school? On my day
off could I go out and see Dr. Ladd? I have written to Dr. but he never
answered my letter yet.

   When there are people more to the east side they said they will give me
more money. It is a nice family I am with. She goes away in the morning
and I don't see her until 3 or later in the afternoon. How are you feeling? I
will get a day off next week and I am going to see my mother. She will tell
you what I said about the pay I am getting. When you go out to the Exeter
School tell the girls that I know I was asking for them. Miss McTernan I
will give you this address where I am at now so if you want to call me here
any time you will find me in.

   Well I will close my short letter by saying by good bye.

From,
Cora Duffy

December 3, 1930

My dear Dr. Ladd,

I am again taking the pleasure in writing to you as I want to tell you
that I am not working on North Main Street any more. I am working on
Glenham Street in a family minding a baby boy three months old and
doing light housework. I am only getting four dollars there but a shop is
going to start up in a few weeks now and the boss said that he will send
me then. I worked there before. I meant to write to you before but been
so tired out and I couldn't find much time. How is Miss Ester and Mrs.
Worden? I am coming out soon and see the attendants there. Tell the
nurse Miss Harris I was asking for her and I thank her, also you, for all that
you both have done for me while I was a patient there. My mother had a
bad fall a few weeks ago. She hurt her arms. Dr. Ladd I am out from the
school five months this December and work so hard. Well Dr. if you think
I write to you too often just tell me and I will not bother then.

   Dr. Ladd I am wishing you and Marion a merry Christmas and a happy
new year. Also the attendants and patients there the same. Dr. Ladd since I
came home now and working I weigh 100 and 48.

Well I will close.

From,
Cora Duffy

March 11, 1931

Dear Dr. Ladd,

Just a few lines to let you know that I am still working every day and I am not running wild any more.

Dr. Ladd you know when I was at the school I had trouble with my side. I am waiting for a bed at the RI Hospital as they are going to operate on me.

Tell Mrs. Harris I was asking for her.

From,
Cora Duffy

March 14, 1931

My dear Cora:

I am glad to know that you are able to work and able to get a job. I hope
that operation you mention won't prove to be a serious one.

  Let me hear from you occasionally. I will deliver your message to Mrs.
Harris.

Very truly yours,
Joseph H. Ladd, Supt.

April 1, 1931

My dear Dr. Griffin:

I wonder if you would send Dr. Ladd a report on the operation on Cora
Peartree (or Duffy, as we know her).

  We had her for several years and last summer she was allowed on
vacation. Since then she has had various jobs and while she is not yet on
the parole list, being still called On Vacation, it would seem that she might
soon be given parole status.

  She was a patient for about two weeks in Ward I prior to being operated
on last Saturday, March 28. She states that her reproductive organs have
been removed but can give no basis for such a statement. Inasmuch as she
has had three illegitimate children such a condition would favor her being
put on parole.

  Any information you will send Dr. Ladd will be much appreciated.

Respectfully,
Miss Mary F. McTernan
Social Worker, Exeter School

April 6, 1931

Dear Dr. Ladd:

Dr. Griffin has asked me to answer a letter written April 1, 1931 by your Social Service worker, Miss Mary F. McTernan in regard to Cora Peartree.

I wish to advise that this patient was admitted to the Rhode Island Hospital on March 16, being referred to us by own Gyn. Out-Patient Department. This patient gave the history of continual pelvic pain. After being observed for a few days by the surgeons on service, it was decided, with her consent, to perform an operation with the possibility of doing a hysterectomy, hoping thereby to relieve her from her symptoms. The patient gave her consent, and the following operation was performed March 28, 1931:-

"Amputation of cervix; perinorraphy; supra-vaginal hysterectomy; double salpingo-oophorectomy and appendectomy."

If there is any further information which you desire, please let me know.

Yours truly,
George Wheatley, M.D.
Assistant Superintendent, Rhode Island Hospital

September 22, 1931

DISCHARGED

Mental Status: Moron
Total Duration of Instituton Life: 7 years, 9 months, 29 days
Reason for Discharge: *No longer a social problem*

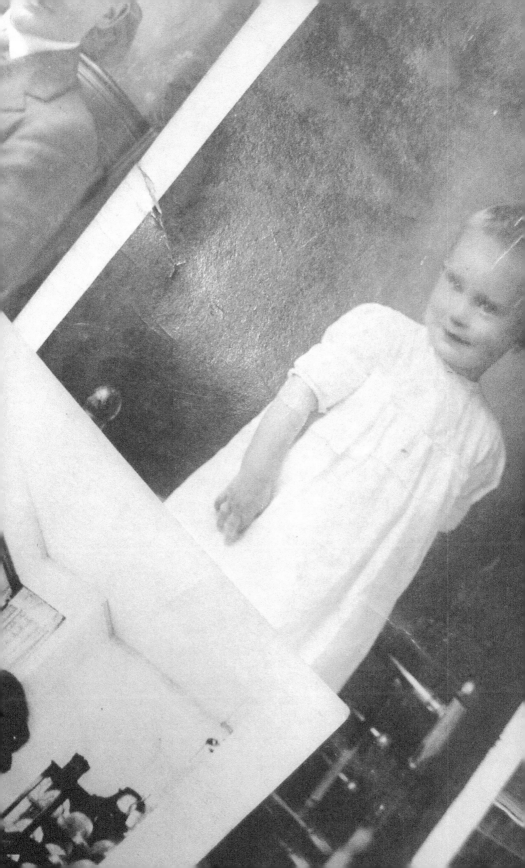

Better Not Born, Better Off Dead

Yet not all the doctor's cases were treated the same. In fact, it was well understood among Exeter girls that some were favored over others. Many were the pleading letters written to Dr. Ladd from the less fortunate ones, begging for their release, claiming they were being detained unfairly, while their less obedient sisters were allowed to return to the community. In fact the children of religious and affluent families, especially, were treated more justly with regard to their liberty, and typically afforded more and greater chances to make good on their promises to amend their immoral ways on the outside.

But perhaps, too, the untimely death of his wife in 1927, the first Mrs. Ladd, had softened the doctor's heart and planted the seed of doubt in his mind that the Exeter School was justified in its practice of institutionalizing women on the basis of their sexuality.

Nevertheless, bound by their duty to "*protect society against nameless children,*" the institution's overseers often proved that their charity ought not be tested. Once under the thumb of state social services, feeble-minded girls and women on parole from the Exeter School, branded by the scarlet letters of defective delinquency and promiscuity, were so ever after haunted by the threat of returning to the institution, and so forced to live in the shadows of shame and fear. And if any untoward activities were brought again to the attention of local authorities, the consequences would be grave indeed.

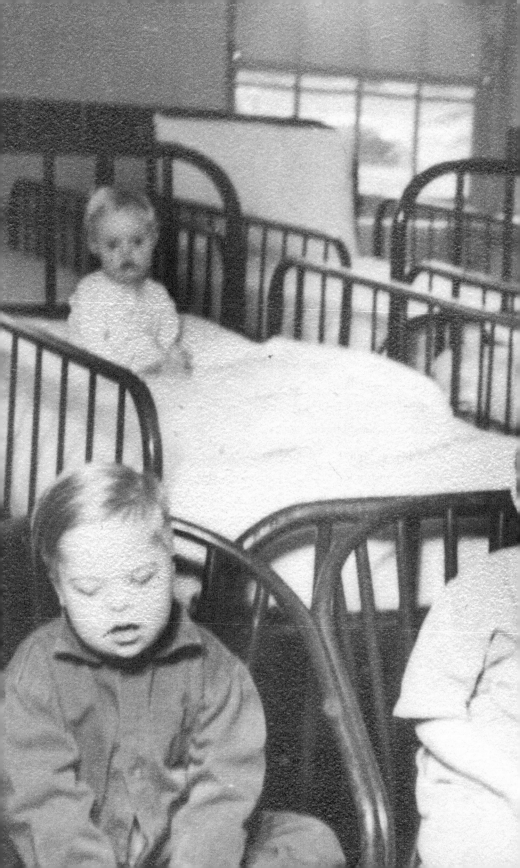

DOROTHY

Dorothy Farmer. Sixteen years old. Mental age nine years. Single. American. Protestant. Moron. Reads and writes. Immoral behavior. Sex promiscuity. Frequented houses of ill fame. Would not go to school. Defective delinquent. Six inches below normal height. Is typically feeble-minded in her poor judgment, comprehension and her general attitude. Both sisters much retarded. Actual residence, Providence. Committed by Sixth District Court. Father died of tuberculosis. Mother remarried. Patient is oldest of three siblings of whom she and another are living with a paternal aunt. Claims to have been assaulted by four Portuguese in a shack on Well Street. Has told of other imaginary assaults including some alleged to have taken place in the Rescue Home and Mission.

December 17, 1927

Dorothy Farmer.

Clothes - clean.

Body - clean.

Head - clean.

Scars - Burn on left leg caused by a fire cracker. Burn on left elbow.

Callouses on both feet.

Clothes.

1 winter shirt.

1 pair winter bloomers.

1 cotton slip, (white).

1 pair stockings

1 Serge dress

1 pair of shoes

1 pair of garters

1 sanitary napkin

Ms. L.S.

January 5, 1928

My dear Dr. Ladd:

Please find enclosed a duplicate copy of our summary on the case of
Dorothy Farmer who was committed to Exeter December 17, 1927. We are
sorry that there has been this delay in getting this summary off to you.

Yours most sincerely,
Dorothy L. Roberts
Social Worker, The Rhode Island Society for Mental Hygiene

March 18, 1928

Dr. Ladd,

I am asking you if I could go once more with my aunt. She is my foster mother. She is the one that needs my help. She has done everything for me. Now I think it's my turn to do my share towards her. I know for the last three months I have been locked up and have not had the chance, and if I can go to her about the first of April I will do great. She also wants my help. She's been good to me, why can't I return my thanks to her?

I am a very good worker here. Also I have been told I am the best behaved girl you have here.

Very much oblige,
Dorothy Farmer

March 21, 1928

My dear Mrs. Farmer:

I examined Dorothy this morning in regard to the appendicitis which she thinks she has. I find she has a sore spot in her side in the vicinity of her appendix. She says that this hurts her when she bends and makes certain movements, but does not give her any pain when she is quiet. Evidently if it is appendicitis it is very mild.

However, I think I will send her out to the hospital and have an examination made of her to see if there really is anything that can be found.

Very truly yours,
Joseph H. Ladd, Supt.

May 8, 1928

My dear Mrs. Farmer:

I have just taken Dorothy to the hospital at the State Infirmary. There is a possibility that she may have appendicitis, thought I am not sure that this is the case.

I would like to have permission, if you please, to operate on her if it becomes necessary.

I took her to the hospital so she might be there in case she suddenly becomes worse and requires an operation immediately. If she does not prove to have appendicitis she will be returned here in a few days.

Very truly yours,
Joseph H. Ladd, Supt.

May 9, 1928

Mr. Joseph H. Ladd,

Dear sir your letter was received and I am very sorry to learn of Dorothy's
illness. If it is absolutely necessary to perform the operation go ahead and
at it, and please give me a permit to see her. I should like to go out and see
her. I would like to go to see her Sunday. Please let me hear from you at
once.

Your truly,
Mrs. Mary Farmer

May 12, 1928

My dear Mrs. Farmer:

Your letter for permission to go and see Dorothy Sunday didn't come until yesterday and I was busy with a committee and was unable to answer it until this morning. However, it will be all right for you to go anyway during visiting hours.

I very much doubt if it is going to be necessary to operate on Dorothy. My opinion is that there isn't much physically wrong with her. I was unable to find anything, but I had no x-ray or anything of that sort for examination while they have an apparatus at Howard. My idea in sending Dorothy out there was that, if against my judgment she did develop appendicitis, she would be there ready for the operation immediately, while if she was here she would have to undergo a long, painful ride to the hospital.

I think Dorothy's trouble is more in the nature of hysteria than it is any physical disease, but, of course, we never can be sure about these things, and it is better to be on the safe side.

Very truly yours,
Joseph H. Ladd, Supt.

May 25, 1928

Dear Dr. Ladd:

I wish to inform you that Dorothy Farmer was operated upon yesterday by
Dr. John Chamberlain Jr. for appendicitis. At this time the patient is in
good condition and fairly comfortable.

Very truly yours,
Karl B. Sturgis, M.D.,
Superintendent, State Infirmary

May 26, 1928

My dear Mrs. Farmer:

Dorothy was operated on for appendicitis on last Thursday, and is in good shape and fairly comfortable.

It will be all right for you to go out to see her at the hospital at the State Infirmary in a few days. You may communicate with Dr. Sturgis.

Very truly yours,
Joseph H. Ladd, Supt.

August 11, 1928

Dear Dorothy:-

I hope you will write to me when ever you can. I love you as much as ever
and think of you often and feel that you are and always will be my little
Dorothy.

   Tell me is Virginia there and Bridget and any of our other girls?

   I had a nice letter from your aunt. I haven't been to RI since the last time
I saw you. When I come again I'll come to see you.

   I have been sick all summer with sties in my eyes. They were very painful
and made me feel sick all over.

   Mrs. Robb is a bad old woman and I have nothing to do with her.

   Be a good girlie and do your best wherever you are in this world and the
Lord will reward you.

   I'll send you post cards that I receive sometimes if you'd like them, would
you?

Yours always,
E.H. Russell

November 7, 1928

Dear Antoinette,

I am very sorry that you and Adeline won't speak to each other. She said you snubbed her and every thing. Now if that's on account of me I am very sorry she always says that you treat her mean. This morning she asked you if you wanted the pictures. You walked right out the door and never answered. Sunday night you promised me something. When I asked you for what your promised you said, "I don't care what I promise." Why did you say that? If it was any body else you would say sure with a smile but you snap my mouth right up. I go along and say nothing about it. I hope you will be at the movies tomorrow night. I missed you last week. I did not enjoy it because you was not there. Please answer soon.

X X X

Sincerely yours,
Dorothy Farmer

October 9, 1929

Dr. Ladd -

Dear sir my daughter Dorothy is anxious to come home and I thought I
would take her home on trial and see how she gets along. If I can have her
I would like to have her on the 24th of October. Will you kindly let me
know at once and greatly oblige her mother.

Mrs. Mary Farmer

October 15, 1929

My dear Mrs. Farmer:

In reply to your note of October 9th concerning taking Dorothy home I would say that it seems to me advisable to let her remain here some time longer.

   We have just had an examination by the psychologist, and from the result of this examination it would appear that Dorothy is not quite ready for parole.

Very truly yours,
Joseph H. Ladd, Supt.

August 17, 1930

Dr. Ladd,

I am well and hope you are the same. I also wish to be remembered to all
that know me. I intended to write to you before this just to thank you for
giving me such a nice vacation. It was a real surprise to me. Now since
I have been home I have got my self a nice place to work and I am ever
getting along quite nice. I am taking care of a little boy about four years
old and he has taken a liking to me. I make five dollars a week. So you see
that's the reason I haven't written before this.

  So if it won't be too much trouble I would very much love to have all my
home clothes and my Boston bag and my jacket. Miss Stone will know just
about where these are. If she doesn't know she can ask one of the girls.
Louise or Gladys. And please have them sent to Winter Street because I
am not at home and the people at Winter Street will see that I get them
when I return from work.

Very much oblige,
Dorothy Farmer

August 30, 1930

Dr. Ladd,

Dear sir, just a line to let you know how my niece Dorothy is getting along.
I have had no trouble with her as yet. She is doing nicely. I would love to
keep her longer if you think best. Please put her on parole and give her a
trial. Mrs. McTurney called to see her yesterday and she thought she was
doing well. Please let me hear from you soon and oblige.

Mrs. Mary Farmer

September 10, 1930

My dear Mrs. Farmer:

I received your letter in regard to Dorothy, and I am very glad Dorothy is doing so well, and hope she will continue to do well.

  We are to have a parole meeting next Thursday, and I have Dorothy's name on the list to be taken up at that time.

  You may plan to keep Dorothy at any rate until you hear from me again.

Very truly yours,
Joseph H. Ladd, Supt.

September 24, 1930

My dear Mrs. Farmer:

The Commission voted to parole Dorothy to your custody, so you are at liberty to keep Dorothy home as long as she conducts herself properly.

Very truly yours,
Joseph H. Ladd, Supt.

May 9, 1931

My dear Dorothy:

I am hearing some little rumors that are more or less disturbing to me on
your account. Possibly these are nothing but rumors, but certainly I hope
that you are not forgetting yourself and are in any danger of doing anything
foolish that you will have to pay for.

Very truly yours,
Joseph H. Ladd, Supt.

May 19, 1931

My dear Dorothy:

I am sorry you were disturbed by the letter I wrote you. Miss McTernan
made a little report about another girl named Farmer, and I took it to be
you.

  Hope you will pardon me this time.

Very truly yours,
Joseph H. Ladd, Supt.

August 11, 1931

Dr Ladd,

I am well and hope you are the same. I am working each day ever I since
I came home. I have been home one year June 30, 1930. I am trying and
working hard to do the things that is right. I have not wrote to you since
I been home. You must think I am a nice one not to do so, but I have
not forgotten you for you have helped me to have this chance and I am
thanking you by not giving any trouble. I wish to be remembered to all the
attendants and girls that I know. Hope all the girls will have a chance like I
did. Auntie sends love to you and I am helping her all I can. I am helping
her by giving her my money and not any trouble.

  I hope I will not be doing anything out the way by asking you if I may
write to Louise Jones and can she write back to me? Also Gladys Sun, can
she write back to me? I would like to hear from them lease. I also want to
thank you for taking your car to carry me to the hospital for my sickness.
They did a nice job on me and was very nice to me. I hope to hear from
you very soon. It has been quite a while since you have wrote to me. I hope
I will be able to write to Louise and Gladys. I thought to ask you first.

From,
Dorothy

September 15, 1931

My dear Dorothy:

I was glad to get your letter and to know you are getting along so nicely and are so happy. You speak of not writing to me previously. Of course, I like to hear from the boys and girls who are out, but I don't expect them to write if they don't feel like it.

I doubt if it is advisable for you to write to Gladys or any of the other girls. It seems to me that the acquaintances which you make here at the school had better be dropped when you get out. That you should try to make the acquaintance of people who possibly can be of some benefit to you.

I hope you will notice I am not saying anything against Gladys, but it seems that it is rather doubtful if Gladys will ever be in a position in which association with her could be of any assistance to you in any way. You see Gladys hasn't always done quite the right thing, and there are lots of people who know about this, and the people who do know about it will quite probably believe that Gladys will always be the same sort of girl. If you associate with her they will consider you to be that same type of girl. It makes but very little difference how well Gladys behaves when she goes back to her home. It will be very difficult to convince these people that she has changed. Once you get a bad name it is very difficult to live it down.

Very truly yours,
Joseph H. Ladd, Supt.

January 11, 1932

Gentlemen:

Some time ago one of our paroled patients, Dorothy Farmer, seemed
to need some attention on account of trouble with a scar following an
operation for appendicitis performed at the State Infirmary. I talked
with Dr. Sturgis and asked Miss McTernan to take the girl out there for
examination, not thinking she would have to remain.

However, she did remain, and in course of examination it was found that
she is pregnant, and I understand she still is there.

Is there any action of the Commission necessary in this case or not?

Very truly yours,
Joseph H. Ladd, Supt.

January 13, 1932

Dear Dr. Ladd,

Based on your recommendation, approval is given to transfer Dorothy
Farmer from Exeter School to the State Infirmary for confinement.

  Will you please give any information you may have regarding the paternity
of her child.

Yours very truly,
Thomas Murphy,
Secretary, State Public Welfare Commission

February 4, 1932

My dear Mr. Murphy:

Sometime ago you wrote me requesting information concerning the
supposed paternity of Dorothy Farmer's prospective child. Miss McTernan
has investigated this matter, and find that putative father of this child is
one Jethro Marsh. He was expelled from the congregation of the Church of
God and Saints on Winter Street where he was living in their campground.
He is 15 years old.

Very truly yours,
Joseph H. Ladd, Supt.

June 21, 1932

Dr. Ladd,

Dear sir I am writing to you in regard of Dorothy Farmer, my niece, which I adopted. In regards to taking her home from the State Infirmary, I know that she has done wrong. But of all that she has asked forgiveness and she has been severely punished, and she has promised me that it would never be the case again. She asked me to give her one more trial and I feel as I should do it. Now I have more help with her than I had before and I think that I will be able to manage her. You know the Lord said in St. Matthew. Chapter 6:14:15 reads like this. Please let me know if you will let me take her so that I can go after her. May the Lord bless you for your kindness. I know that you are a man of consideration. She is all that I have in the world and I feel as though I should try to make a nice young lady of her, if she will hear me, as I am of a strict religion and believe in doing what is right living and letting live.

Anxiously waiting to hear from you.

Respectfully yours,
Mrs. Mary Farmer

June 26, 1932

My dear Mrs. Farmer:

I will take up the matter of Dorothy coming home at the next meeting.

I saw Dorothy at the State Infirmary yesterday, and she told me she wanted to go out. I said, "Then you don't want to go back to the school." She said, "I suppose I have been bad enough to deserve to." I told her we would not bring her back to the school because she had been bad but to prevent her being bad again. I told her if she thought she had had enough of that sort of thing and could walk straight hereafter, we didn't want her to come back to the school.

However, we will consider her at the next parole meeting.

Very truly yours,
Joseph H. Ladd, Supt.

August 11, 1932

My dear Mrs. Farmer:

It was voted at the parole meeting to allow Dorothy to go home with you.

Very truly yours,
Joseph H. Ladd, Supt.

April 18, 1933

Dear Dr. Ladd,

Dorothy Farmer, now on parole from Exeter School, is to be admitted to the State Infirmary because of pregnancy.

Yours very truly,
Thomas Murphy
Secretary, State Public Welfare Commission

August 16, 1933

Dear Dr. Ladd:

It is necessary for me to inform you that Dr. Harold Isabel, Visiting
Obstetrician, has seen and examined Dorothy Farmer during her period
at the Institution. He arranged to do a cesarean, which he did yesterday to
terminate pregnancy.

She was in her usual condition up to the time of the operation. She was
operated upon yesterday forenoon and during the operation she developed
a sudden heart condition. She failed rapidly and passed away in the
operating room.

Her aunt and mother were notified and made arrangements for the
remains. The infant died at the same time.

Very truly yours,
Karl B. Sturgis,
Superintendent, State Infirmary

August 17, 1933

DISCHARGED

Mental Status: Moron
Total Duration of Institution Life: 5 years, 8 months
Reason for Discharge: *Death by child birth*

EXETER GIRLS

Made in United States
North Haven, CT
15 March 2024

50018149R00161